SCATTER

Written and with illustrations by You-You Ma

Island North Press

New York

First edition, 2015

The Library of Congress has catalogued the softcover edition as follows:
Ma, You-You
ISBN 978-0-692-45910-2

Illustrations and Cover Design by You-You Ma

Printed in the United States of America.

to m & d
& all my inspirations
...
for always letting me see the light

CONTENTS

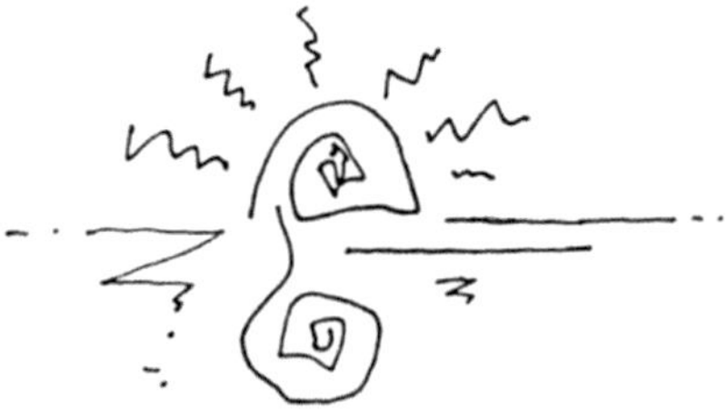

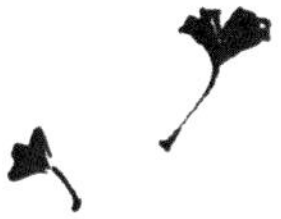

How to capture ephemerality, or the infinity of a single moment?
(like a cloth of twilight caught in a jar of fireflies in summer...)
Once past, now gone. A train whooshing past a platform in September. somewhere between these covers is a collection of such singular moments—raw, unedited, strange, unfiltered by light, un-tonguetied by syntax or convention…

a sc a
t t er
i n g of paper leaves, falling from an orchard cathedral like that day, arms outstretched, collecting them as they fell, one by one, from the sky...ephemerality singing its original loose and lonely form. Collected, a story. A story but also a diary—one unconscious of itself. so it is to let loose into someone else's mind, not from intention but simply from sensation: images, sounds, smells...the sea. sheer distillation of the unfiltered mind.

It is to capture but never fully capture the freedom of that sensation, forever scattered, singing, its little footsteps across the sand…

~ *Centerport, New York, Sept. 2014*

SCATTER

SOUNDLESS SEA

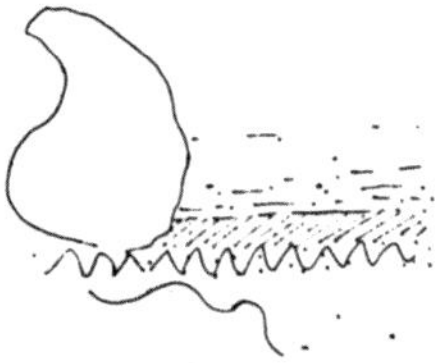

consummate
the cove & the
shore . . .

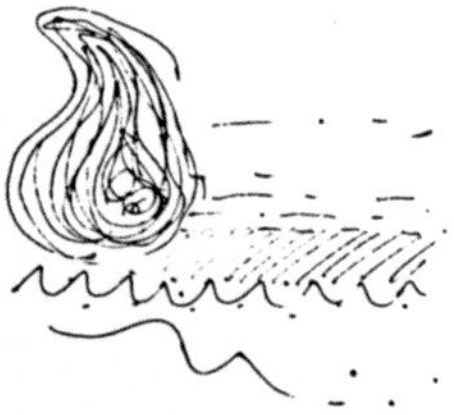

soundless glide

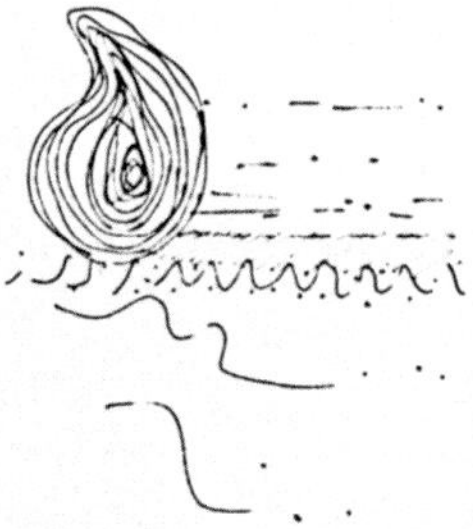

synonymous . . .
one skin & the sand . . .

ynonymous

It has all become
s y n o n y m o u s:
the wind with the rain,
our skin with the sand,
our thoughts
and
the solemn stoicism
of the black rochers that soundless glide,

invisible evenings beneath
la
lune,
the
softness
& the
sound.

Valley of broken glass still beautiful

Ceiling art is such, so that staring, white grains become white sands become ocean floor become fossilized dreams become fibrous plants become caravan serenade… as the night closes in on me, color draining away like paint from this world I see everything turning yet it all stays still, and I hold my breath—to the command of some hushed whisper deep inside telling me to wait before I close my eyes to sleep…

Standing on a high wire taut as overstretched overimagined but-not-overlived string I am looking down at everything I once thought I would have but which truth had conquered in a wellfoughtwar, this valley of broken glass still beautiful and singing its loose broken parts,

fragments in the sun.

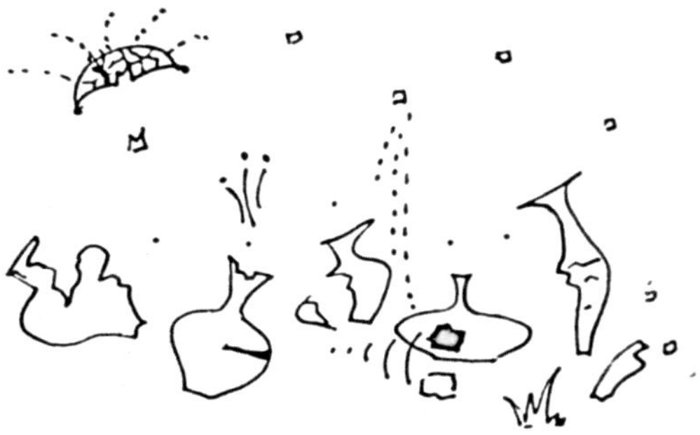

White sands

Earlytidestrolling to the lighthouses that gradually fade away, like little ghosts that follow the footsteps of shipwrecks only to get lost again in campfire evenings adrift with songs asunder; so we set out to find in the one farthest away along the shore, the lighthouse with one eye, the one that greedily houses the vestiges of old dawns dancing in its cupboards de l'ombre des vagues luminescentes, afternoons aglow with fragrant wood, staircases that climb up backwards to moonrise and sunrise but not to heaven, and us coming up and gasping for breath and asking: do you smell the sweetness of the salt, like a long lost traveler coming in? We opened the cupboards one by one, as the luminescent waves came up and started to dance by shadows untempted, as the sundrops came up and erased our path down again—white sands of morning and white sands of time, and to find ourselves suddenly disoriented, like strangers arising in a foreign land—

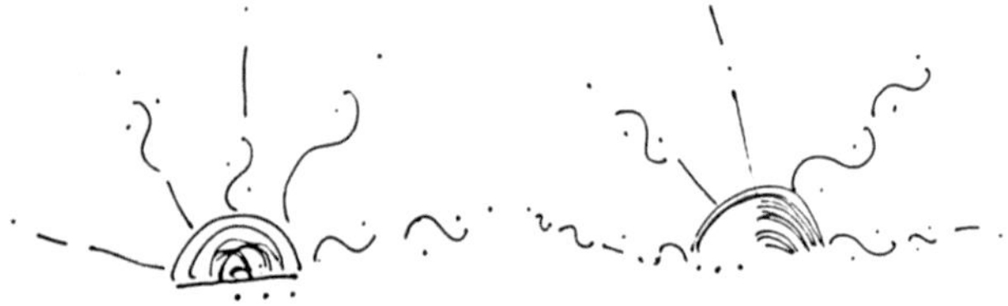

ky-singing

She's singing the sky, and the endless illusion. the rhythm of repetition, the repetition of rhythm; the chasm, the connection that binds and fixes.

i see everything from my panorama of clouds, an arch beneath my straw-brimmed hat, a constant reminder that the earth is round; there's the gray sand, gray ocean, sun-tipped wings of albatross flying low overhead, and of course, Nabokov's mots, This is exactly how I imagined paradiso…the endless vagues, the slow blossoming of clouds, the calm minus the emptiness. somewhere you don't even realize the sound of the sea, because it all blends into one experience: at the same moment, at every moment, if you somehow manage to le garder inside. like seashells.

i heard once, that the sea has many voices. one that beckons, one that forbids, one that gives fear, and one that gives calm; one that preserves and one to destroy, one to keep time, one that loses time, one in order to forgive, and one so to forget. and so she said, the sea with its so many voices must be so many people; so many people, voices, storms and dawns.

On antelopes & flamingos

I have tried to think so much…to reign it in. As if I were standing on top the precipice, looking down—and they'd all be there, those damn antelope men and flamingo women.

There's nothing I want more than a purge of all these meaningless sighs, the way they take up so much room, and leave us breathless…

There's really nothing more to be said. The whole room is filled to the brim with these wet sighs like wet inescapable seas. Dreams of other colors, our unfulfilled plastic desires, of fuchsia and brown, of other unlived moments

that cling to me, stick to me, on my clothes, seep into me.

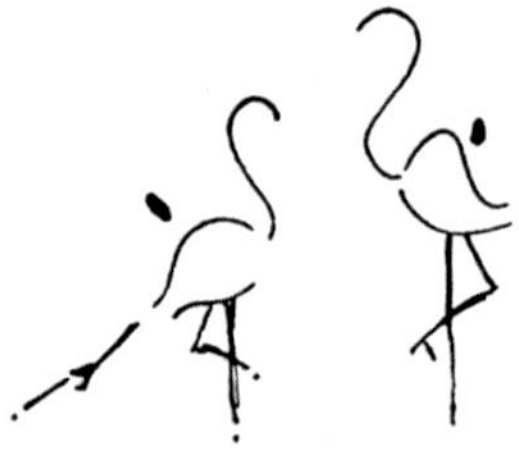

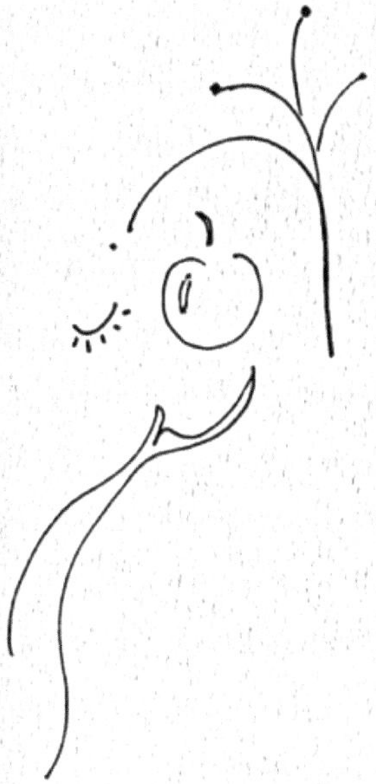

Shifting. standing. shivering. on one foot to another. Gray skies reflected in one shard of glass held in our gloved hands and as much as we wanted to we couldn't release and let it go—

the pine cones folding in one on top the other

and we couldn't drop it on the floor and let it shatter, into a thousand broken skies like broken hearts smaller and smaller like the remnants of a bullet into skin as it scatters disperses like dandelions at the start of autumn, sur la colline où l'eglise stands of stone and sand, blue-gray liquid of souls stood solemn like eyes—And always, the pines overhead, scribbling circles their soft flesh fanning out like stars—it appeared in a shard of glass as I held it up to catch the light to catch in song what trespassed of the white apple down of the last chords of summer in flight going down south to my prenatal voyage to find a lost chord of an ending created in a cabin sheltered by pines where our hands conjoined finally could, in the last epithet of eternity and old age, grasp such illusions of the mauve glass-green of sea bottles forgotten and the blue-gone-silver of forgotten dawns…

Shoreline of "Forgotten"

Tonight I am filled, with whispers from the clovers in the husky field at twilight.
They resonate with such tender glow
as if from some distant somber sound echoing from the barge near where
shadow-boats sway,
lethargic, to some song once known but forgotten by man,
in a harbor filled with such quiescence,
almost like emptiness on a page.

When Night rests his fallen fingers on the old man's beard, when the tide has
crumbled away piece by piece to lay decrepit at the shore,
this is when they come

on little clothed feet,
and force me to remember who I am.

To trace these sand-filled footsteps back, is hard, when the going is backwards
against the pull of the gravity of Time; but even harder for them, to trek across the
emptiness—

How dare they—impose upon the solitude behind which I hide
expose these sins to a world that cares no more
than to bring me mortal errands on a silver-gilded plate. And yet
we are still running and drying
like innocent clockwork-tides. I wrap my shawl
around me, as I slowly trace

this shoreline named "forgotten",
realizing as I taste the bitter wind that soon
I will be leaving for another city. Easy it would be
to be happy against the curse of angels,

happy to just be forgetting.

Yolanda

And we saw that the early tides brought in stuff beyond the ordinary smells of saltine sea, rubber boots, or the old used nets lost by some other fisherman some other year; sometimes in the backdrop of cloudygraybluеindigo close to the lighthouse with one eye they bring in the orange stuff of last summer's dream, or even several ago, smells of Yolanda's hair crisp and golden, apple trees and silver skies overlooking all signs of the city ignored;

I like to sit there, by the edge, on the rock by the place where they sell their wares, on the shores of Salina, with the song and the sky, a poet, and a postman who knows his name; it is like a futbol game, this waiting, for a goal that you don't know when it will come, this patience for a thing you know shall come—harder to catch than fish; it comes and goes.

ɔllecting

At the shore
Looking at the boy who collects rocks
And she asked

So what do you collect?
and I said,
memories, I collect memories.

smoldering

the steam from my mug
transcended
filtering up
I grow a beard
as I am caught growing old,
listening

Downstairs, even the
radio
          breathes fumes

and I am caught
smoldering
on a pyre of my own making

Horn | Ivory

And it was always horn | ivory, horn into ivory, the cornucopia of our inverted desires; orange leaves upon olive faded gray, ashes and wine scattered across dry wind, diverting in size in the mausoleum of funhouse mirrors; always one to release all truths | the other to release all dreams into reality…and then what of you? you had scattered my ashes into the river and forgot to think about me once you turned your back to the swollen river swollen like a vein gray and throbbing like a pulsing fish swelling up with internal water upon sand; such displays as the mirrors would see diverting sizes and shrinking truths until they became insignificant and swelling up illusion to fill papa's shoes the leather ones in the closet shadow by the garage entrance with the cat door flap shoes that leave a hole on the sidewalk with each step, for isn't it true that those who know us best know us least?

—and what of me? Still thinking of you with every scattered ash of me throbbing scattered separated not even into strands separated into separate separate pieces unable to connect their parts but still ever searching not for themselves but for you, scattered ash throbbing like a school of seawater fireflies drowning in alarm blinking in synchronization even as the limp hard body itself is calcified into coral into stone and I could no longer feel or much less imagine the cool evening breeze filtering over and through my naked skin the way it always had on all the evenings before I slept as I emptied out my mind only to fill it—cannot no longer and the dinophyta is no longer glowing but only a shell-life uninhabited upon the shore as if it contained only air yet we had indeed seen the oceans and the sands and the island of the olive and orange groves, and *what of us*? only the illusion something to show but to show is to mock or to show is to off, only the illusion that can show but cannot speak

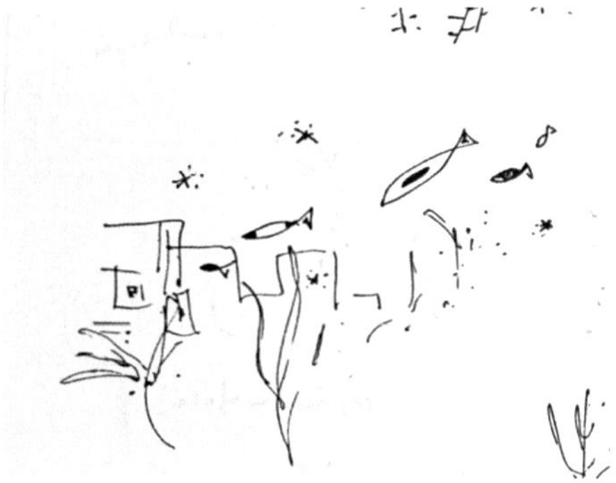

Into smoke…

She had seen that blue only once before. stood on top of a cliff looking down. it had scared her then. she couldn't remember why exactly. interminable blue of smoke and smolder…this time, she was facing backwards to the forest, the cliff of the known all of a sudden the lesser known and the unfamiliar suddenly the un-strange: Arrowhead of her arms draws a circle to the top and her fingers touch at a pinnacle-point…

To let go, as if we were succumbing to smoke—simultaneously with purpose yet un-purposefully, as if we no longer had a choice. yet, it couldn't have been another—there was no one to push us into the abyss or to let us go. Only ourselves. and the only thing that was certain was that there was no one to catch us if we fell.

it is like letting go into a sky with all the weight of sinking, sinking ship and sinking soul shrinking shadows and sinking shadows; simultaneously letting go and succumbing condensing into our heavy lugubrious sins. sinking and falling all at once, one motion, one gesture, a sweep of eternity in some-say grace-full gesture carrying with it its own chains.

She sat—glistening—washing her feet by the lake, not knowing that water is an impure medium it takes the form of tears. Sometimes the scales of cold fish. Stories and songs unspoken.

Pass on, the ephemerality of all perished things, even though they live on in our memory, long after they are gone, long after the petals are crushed and broken, long after the ghosts of Sylvia and the transients have left on Tuesday's afternoon train. They move on, although they live on, somewhere, beyond the grass plains—Ephemeral, yet forever, infiltrating our current state, and leaving scars or sustaining us alive, such influx of imaginations, like a sky constructed of paper wings…

Imagine for a second, if we were, to construct a sky out of the land of perished things… for which faces ingrained; which smells imprinted; which essence of once-flowering leaves; which motion and gravity…

Of course, he was still south, at the foot of the bridge—wavering in her memory, the tide cold and falling like the paint of the graffiti of lovers chipping away. along the stucco, down by the old canal, she walked alone.

For it was green

For it was green, all green,
like the little spurt in the lungs the moment you surface up for air. the paper algae, and a horse
who is drowning, to the sound of a purple mandolin
left reverbing after the flutterings of the sun. somewhere
swim fish and blue begonias
and colors that smelled like symbolism
counting the days after his leaving, closer to our own dying and his return
for after the rains we were left swimming
left swimming like a dancer falling from the sky
or circling the dining room table
For somewhere there were flowers, and a sea we could not see, smelling like Turkish roses
It doesn't hold you close when you cry or answer your questions when you ask
only leaves you bleeding
the long end of a cigarette, a thought left upended, suspended, as quietest as ever
a composition dangling from an orchard cathedral, singing quietly
on the mornings that have us feeling the absence
sitting still at the breakfast table
and still you dream of a dancer who is swimming and falling from the sky
those smoky unlived moments
and we are but one, and free
as free and scattered
as yellow ginkgos

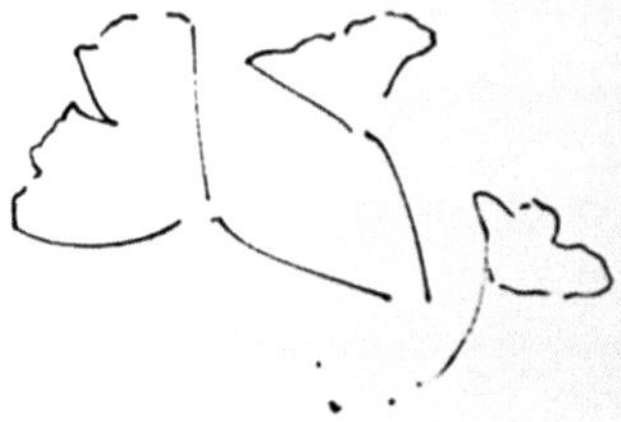

BOOK OF QUESTIONS

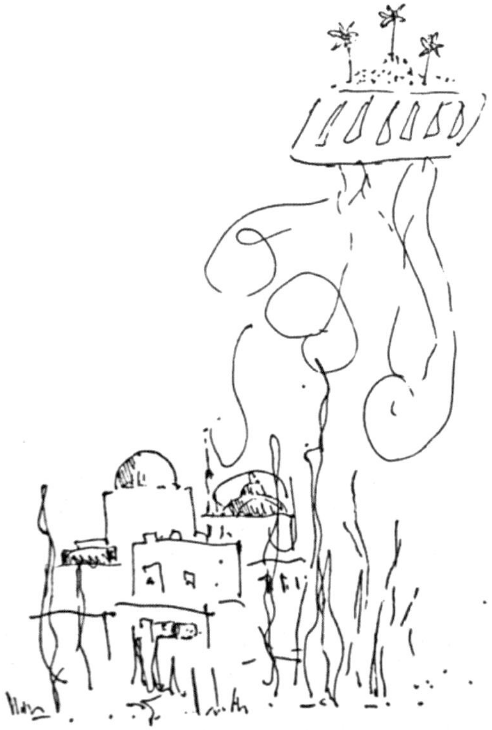

e commencement

Sewers end; slowly tell me, where does sky start?

Ceiling shaking

You looked up, shook your head a bit, smiled at the ceiling. Pourquoi? Quelles étaient tes pensées?

You stood there on the stairway-suspended and smiled at the ceiling shaking your head cursing the day. And I had continued walking on letting you be, which is always the way I am around you, considering innocence a victory until it suffers. And I had only remembered to ask once I got home and it was too late to ask:

Only why were you shaking your head at the ceiling and smiling?

And stranger—maybe the moment has passed. Perhaps tu m'aimais but tu ne m'aimes plus. And now it is I, smiling at the ceiling, cursing the year.

like ink like smoke

It is
like ink
like smoke
like gasoline
inscripted
intangible
unforgettable
order
to disorder
to getting lost without fences
on the page
up to letting go
and sinking to the confines of
a room
without
a key?

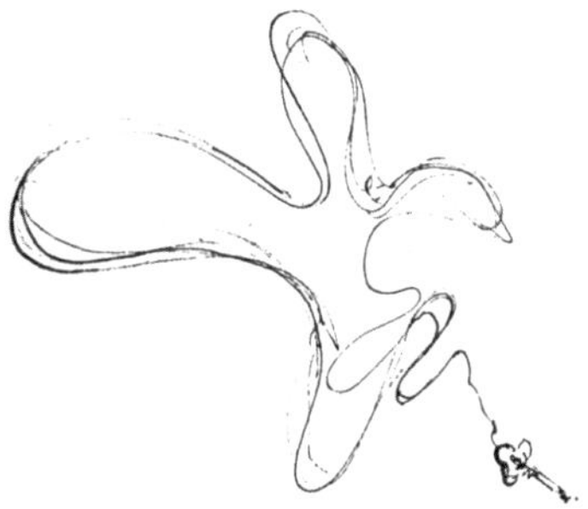

Imperfection

To expose ourselves. To
          Expose ourselves to the colors
To expose ourselves to the—

To expose ourselves to the possibility of imperfection, of the splitting up of parts, of cohesion gone wrong; no Frankenstein glue to put us back together on a shelf, with our pages and our pens. Yet isn't the goal to complete an oeuvre, to cohere all fragments and pieces into one unified being as complete as the perfection of the human form? Or is it instead to fall apart, canyons
                                        into sand?

pilgrimage of the mind

"The feet must become heavy, for the soul to become light." –Unesco Courier

Do we first have to experience physically, all that we seek internally in a pilgrimage of the mind?

And what constitutes a physical experience—one processed through our senses, such as sight and touch, or can a purely inner experience also account for, or create, a physical one?

Suffusing

Gathering petals
preserving the essence
of one flower

Scattering the dust
suffuses and diffuses
sun into air…

…

If we gathered up all the petals scattered on the ground, could we preserve the essence of a flowering tree better than one full flower could? If we gathered it up, and scattered its dust traces on everything, let it suffuse and diffuse from sun into air?

It is…to come and to succumb. Suh-come.

Although physical connection does not occur, do we leave exhausted in collapse, or is there something substantial in the invisible, like in the touch that lies suspended your fingers grazing the air above my skin but not the skin itself or the tension like two poles repelling so strongly they must belong together the tension between two lips infinitely close but have yet to meet one interlocking lip perfectly spaced above the other?

Like a crescent-shaped smile that reaches one ear and falls down in a shiver…

On the ephemeral eternal

if ephemerality is the closest we'll ever get to eternity,
could I say that perhaps fragmentation is the closest we'll get to coherence, to unity?

halk upon the sidewalks

"and she's still, like me…
playing around in the
storm, searching for an answer among the leaves—
or perhaps—just a prayer—caught in the wind and sifting around like a fog:

like clouds on the sidewalks, until the
children disperse of them

chalk on their fingertips

For isn't it true—
she's still, like us
searching around for an answer in the storm—
even if it's just a prayer for an answer?"

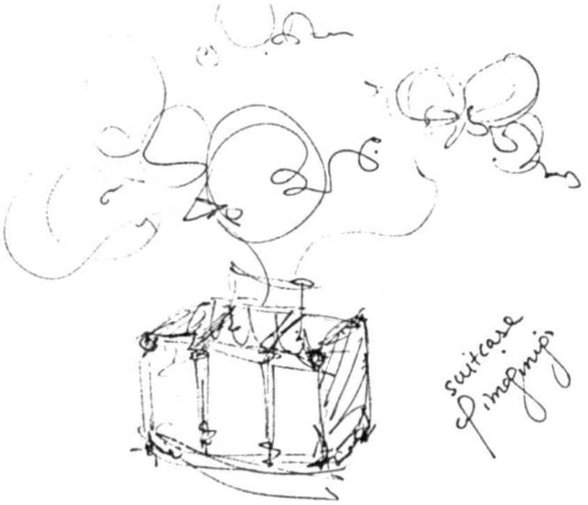

Early mornings

Early morning smells of engine fuel, an irrevocable underpalate of pungent sweetness, of strange grassy green, freshly cut and erupting in a cardamom spritz of early morningmist, something of spiderwebs and dewdelicate as a whisper—it nauseates me sweetly. Under the shade of the linden trees and between the leaves it brings me back to childhood again as I stood je me suis attendue the yellow bus qui exhales soft smoke putt putt like cigar rings into the air… o O O

The fingers extending from the leaves drawing white lines across the sky taking the place of clouds.

Somewhere down the line of gravel impressed, she looks up, traces the smoke, sees her past take shape. the white wisps traced by leaves they too take the shape of clouds. If clouds are symbols of our childhood imaginations, isn't the past, in our old age, only a creation of our imaginations?

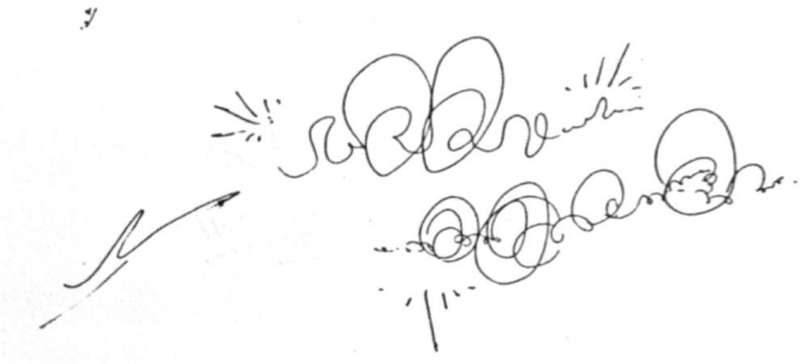

ecember rain

December rain is such a tease
—Such a tease—
Such a pull of unsettling
Uncertainty.
What to do, when all has
been done, and only December rain
left to keep?

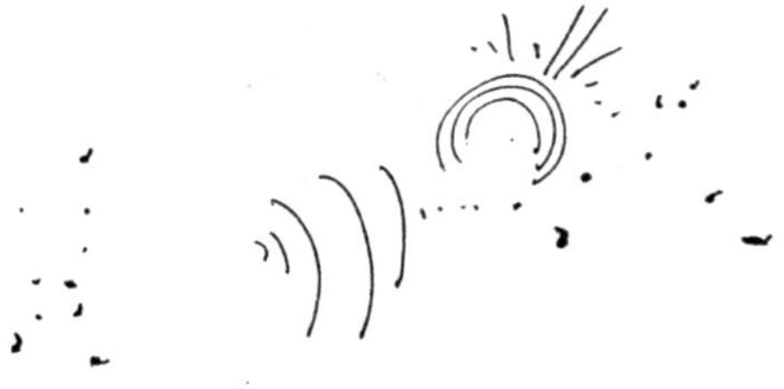

The question persisted—by naming a tangible thing after an intangible thing or things, do we render a concrete thing more impalpable, into the realm of the obscure and of the crepuscule? or do we instead make it more real…

acknowledging the fact that there is something of the crepuscule in all of us, just as there is a mist underlying every day of soleil, a moon for every sun, an invisible skin that feels on top of a visible skin that touches one that shivers at an equally invisible sensation, that hurts and cries and ponders—

> a ghost of the other skin, the latter which, if painted with color, is the only one that others see?

Dear pavement sleeper,

Oh dear pavement sleeper—
are you the one they say who mistakes lampposts for stars?

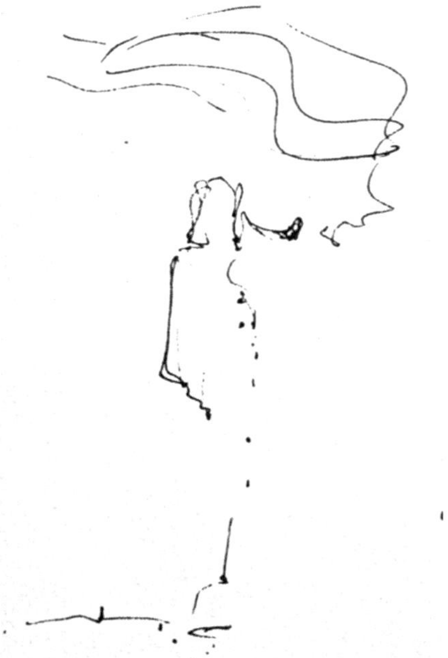

So softlyspeaking of ashes gray on some distant colline where lie layers of dreamtrees the color of raisins soaked in rain

They could not erode their irreversible qualities of age and of death despite the illusion, however true, of that life-giving juicysweetness fruityliquid sense of life erupting all at once like a perfume and a volcano to envelop you in fumes of crackling flowers, of smoldering ashes

Tell me, how could I repent, in what I didn't do, find grace in injustice, embrace all that gives me sorrow?

On se perde, on se trouve…

Getting lost is the same as getting found as I saw in-between two coffees a dime in air it glints like a swipe of dew on ceramic silhouettes tracing the outline of coffee cups like an ice skater the light glimmered caught beneath the lamps overhead turned the other way like sunflowers their heads toward a goal they believed in and at the moment there was no one to prove to them otherwise; as faces danced like shadows inversed so that they were not faces any longer but simply motion freezefrozen in space or perhaps space heatswaying softly to a distant rhyme a journey incomplete along a road with no destination as the embers slowly disappear and re-rise re-arise ghosts from the ashes I see in the reflection an image incomplete—dis-moi, is it her face? As it slowly emerges I see that it is also a part of mine strange how a part of it is moving to the rhythm of grandma's music box strange and soft la musique not of the night but music de la poussière and the other is shifting to an echo of a beat alive out on the streets but dying inside and strange to think

that the hardest thing to do in life is to make friends with a stranger in a filled café even if both of you are lost, even if both of you are found, even if both of you are sitting alone in orbs condensed your own lonely thoughts ready to spill out into another strange to think as you watch his face grow old before your eyes as you stop to catch the writer and winter both inside back bent down arched so lost in thought as liquid seconds drip on goes on drapes over like a curtain in summer as it falls across and onto the hardwood floors de ta jeunesse, as you gazed up swimming in the mirages of light that left everything in D7 chords of special afternoon light such days spent catching fireflies catching time and capturing them into a jar…who could have known that we had labeled them "en ce moment" and "saved for later" when indeed we were, sans savait, catching fireflies catching time, si l'on pouvait, pour la tendre-vieillesse? and you stay longer than you thought you ever could, sitting there mind-shuffling like a fool, curious if you were brave enough to go back and open the jars you pretended to have forgotten—does it smell just as strong as when he had come and made a joke of everything that day

that day of paper clocks and sudden begonias? and the memories still left as strong as the events-unfolded, distorted, like psychedelic arts haunted by experience, or simply faded by sun in a warmer glow…or is it, is it simply fleeting? As the stranger gets up to go you ask if perhaps it had all been inside your own head the winter that was inside too late to know because the only winter that existed was the cold to which you had return and so everything in life that is beautiful is so often short-lived and always uncertain. (Just like second movements in Beethoven, said a little voice) but was it time to go? So the melody dries and the ballerina unwinds but still vous ne savez pas if the answer was to get up and find the answer that cannot be found or to arbitrarily choose one single thing de me vouer, or to simply simply leave everything unfinished as it is…

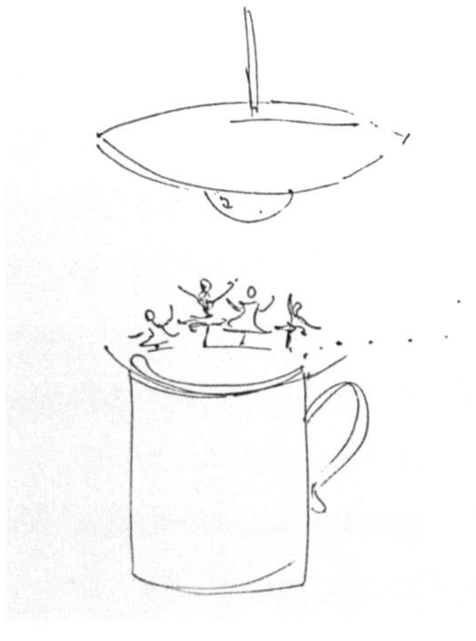

Expiration date

Perhaps that's just the way it is: the next day, it was shriveled up, lying crippled on the table, like a broken flower in a vase without any sustenance. I couldn't remember if and when I had crumbled it.

Because everything has an expiration date.

Sometimes I think of something of importance to say to someone, not with the importance of urgency but rather that of feeling, yet the idea having been thought out too soon, when the moment to say it comes, the feeling that gave life to the phrase lies limp and expires. Soundless cloud without a storm.

Two trains passing and never meeting.

Thought out afterwards, the idea lies fresh but tragically, the moment to say it has gone. It too, had expired long ago and you had somehow blocked it out of consciousness.

Two times conversing but never intersecting—is our love too, one to expire? To expire, like two breaths against the windowpane? Condensing without lasting. To expire, to transpire. Like candles or two flames hushed by a silent wind against an eve sans stars…

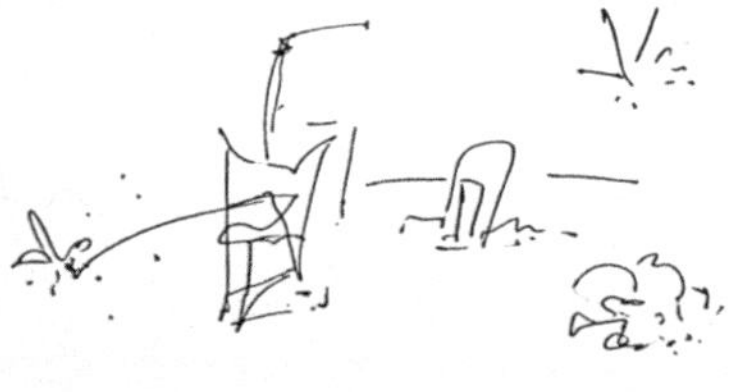

"elegies | laments"
inscribed on a lamppost by the crossing. Street lights screaming, silently. I stand. The white painted bars contrasting the black iron bars. Enfrente de mi, detrás de black iron gates, stood five men who huddled, black suits, conversing. Conversing, the converse of singing. Solemn, like sky is. Only iron bars and white bars separate ellos de mi. Yet who is trapped inside, and who is grieving?

Does futility look different from the outside-in than from the inside-out?

oots

Why are roots beneath the ground, when all they do, is mimic inverseroots—the ones that grow up toward sky?

So we are searching, prime flying, soaring on thin fringes of gray, up dizzying up free from substance but soaring like helium all the same, for something anchored deep into the ground;

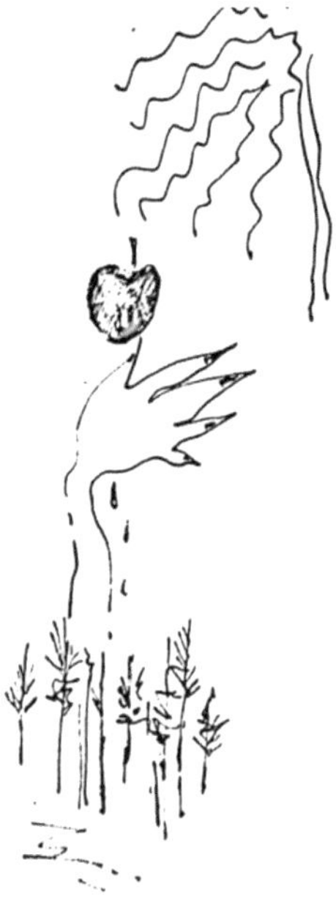

Someone in my dream said the other day, a dream of green and azur, called them “des racines”, yet I didn’t understand what she meant as she grabbed the apple from the orchard keen with green, for deeds done but not admitted, and not learned but always repeated, for thoughts unspoken but guiltily understood, for sins un-committed but attempted, for songs unsung but seen by the skin, and the skin only. How could we know? If but one story and one story only, said Steinbeck from a corner of his eye…the fruit is ripe but an unseemly color; attempt to feel it, and it disappears into the skeins of your hands; lose it, and gain it forever invisible…yet the sun is still out…

And so we disappear into the forest now, as if on an errand or just to cacher les esprits—except this time there is no little box to store our cœurs, or even a little sigh of a lock to store our curiosities. Deep dense deep and there is a clearing with two seats in conversation a curtain of light drawing close yet still we do not stop there deep dark deep light as it is, it is easy to lose ourselves, the first step never the easiest but the easiest if intentionally attempted, the others following in echo momentum like little drums of footsteps that escape the light in synchronized beating, like that of a cœur let loose and still walking on two legs. Into the clearing now, yet not so soon, there is a lady on horseback disrupting the silence—

She is coming toward you now and perhaps farther away, she too is searching for something; the winged onward momentum of her gallop clashes with your own as so often *life is the traveling of two distances opposed*…She is the uncolored rider, as the trees drip away into the gray ink from which they are created; Quick, she is coming fast now, only the color of the berries in the bushes stay sharp plastered on and undrained by the brush of monochrome but they lose their taste—dull wisdom of temptation—the acidity of a colorful life turned bitter on the other side of sweet: it punctures you sans pensées, sharper than sour, and searching for satisfaction, il n'existe plus—

j'en ai assez.

Stranded

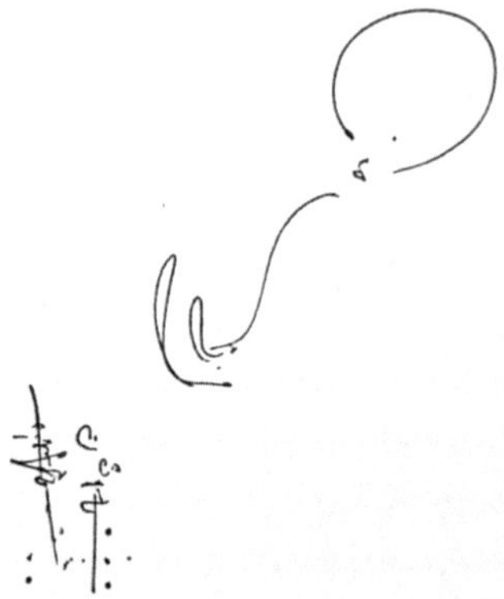

There I was once again stranded, on une plage where the salt was synonymous with sand just when I had thought I had driven my boat far enough out to sea past the origami albatrosses of our own making So my sundried crisp of a soul had separated itself and left light as a piece of paper full of the simplicity of white adobe houses and blue windows reflected seeking the calm so calm where there only existed impossibility—impossibility of a face that solitary ubiquitous face that eternal storm captured at once in the light then in the dark of the undrying waves Has it sunken? That image I mean. Search for that smile those eyes the intricacies contained in that smell search between the seaweeds and between the cracks is it sunken along with the rain that fittingly washes away every Thursday's sins? Perhaps the sins are hiding perhaps they simply go away just like a face that will one day smile eyes without a name.

Is it true that the sins are hiding? Is it true that they simply go away just like a face that will one day smile, eyes without a name?

...Slowly tell me, that where the sewers end, is that the same spot where sky starts? I had cut my strings and learned to forget how to tie the knot that will bring me back to anchor—only the sky, the restless sky that will put me to peace yet perhaps it is all continuum—the good stormed away by the sad the sad cloudpoured down to the bowels of the earth where one day azaleas foxgloves and tender little bleeding hearts will grow up from the strange acid-based-fertilizer of our tears Funny how we always end up with the same conclusion regardless if we start from same or different places regardless if we had gotten lost in the field or stranded inside ourselves. Just like the conclusion that love is a game but one un-admitted to for the sake of preserving that "altar of blame" like you said, but always a continuum, because it's the closest circle round to being forgiven.

Coeurs Comme Bamiyan

It is a cave like my heart that once held and is empty…I didn't let it go but something exogenous stole from it a thing—not born—but created out of its nature. Even stone has a soul has a shape has a pulse that runs profound like the river that streams through its consciousness; years and years it's been yet people still don't see, ages crossed and covered…somewhere someone will see the crash, see the sound once existing now stolen, and now only the silence scattered invisible like the stones that lay beneath my feet—some sort of sentence, like the widows standing in a rubble of their own stoning, but not for love of yourself but for love of "other"… Strange as customs are, the bamiyan buddhas show how our confusion often leaves us destroying our own. How could we be so blind even when our eyes are open? so I speak yet I speak in silence—because the stone holds no sculpture no soul but only the space where it once stood: the structure as the invisible carcass of structure but not the structure itself…Could space exist as space itself and not as the absence of other?

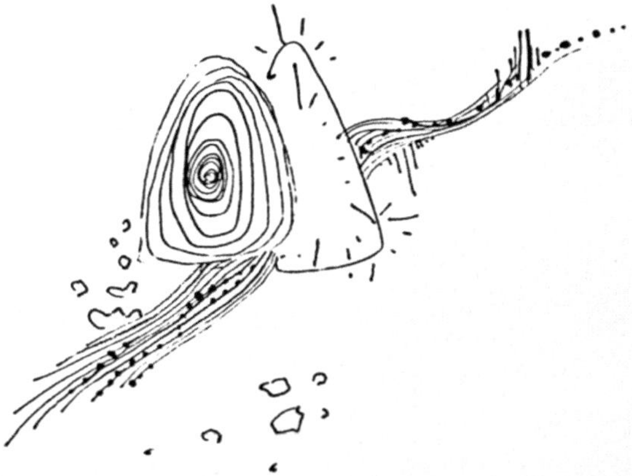

Saccharine smile

…and what is it you are thinking, o precarious thinker? Su corazón a cliff from where the little people of your restless mind dangle, only to be someday blown away by Boreas or scattered like dandelions by Zephyr of the saccharine smile...little oars swimming against the current,

drifting,

if only to fall?

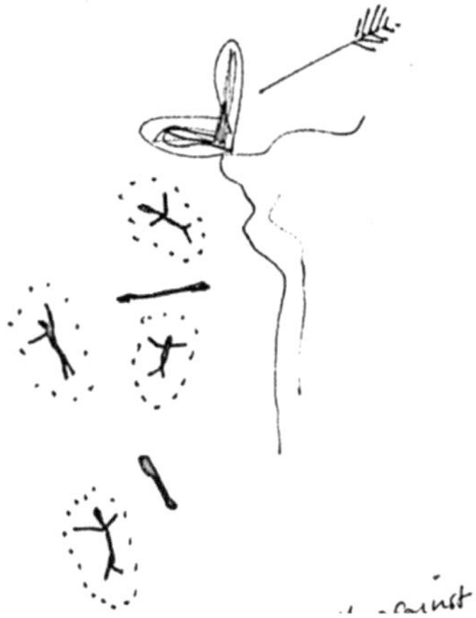

why do we seek loneliness?
is it because it brings us closer to truth, or because it brings us closer to illusion and everything we have dreamed of and still dream of?

Change, like a chameleon

does change, like a carnation, like a chameleon, allow us to see?

Lacking the essence of what was real, we invent our own…we zoom off into the distance of the desert sky invented and laugh with a shriek of a cry, act without thinking to become smaller than small, one little speck against the infinite; speed as in a game of tag with "forever", we house our heart in a house of cards and seek shelter from simply not being seen…but could we really live in a house of cardboard without doubting the strength of these paper walls?

Soon sky-riding silk-kerchief-flying toward that distant horizon speck of that castle we once painted in her basement that summer's eve as it approaches closer as we get farther away from the corrupted metal of our civilization now dense and cold to the touch we seek what we cannot feel but at least we can see it but what is real may be no longer and what does speed taste like? Is it, the air that passes, the intangible, the space, or, all the outposts the deserts the cactus the sunburns the broken tires the canyons the windblown tears the camp-under-stars the armadillos de los stories? The concrete or los colores that we try to grasp and taste along the side of the journey but that which we cannot hold any longer in our hands…Oh friend, catch one for me, an eternity or a day, speed along back so I can taste a moment of your speed speeding along beside me along a stretch of lonelydust singingofstardust such fabric of sleepless canyons, as I continue this life, as it goes by slowly.

Seen and understood

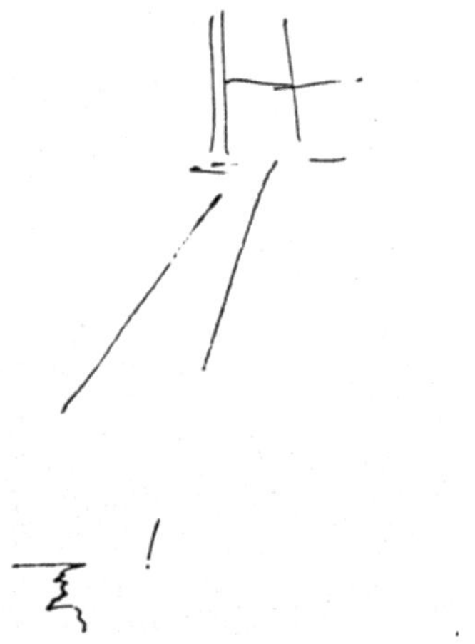

: image I snapped of the sunlight slipping through and staring up from speckled linoleum; It slipped through the wood and the iron hinges of the stall in McCosh 40 around 2pm; and it was a strange light, pale yellow and glowing as if it were smiling a wry smile, a demon or angel amidst the interior darkness, stood and smiled, as if prompting a response or at least a promise to be remembered:

"To be seen and remembered, and not to be seen and understood"—

It stood there and smiled.

And is it really the same for people, is it really a joy to be seen and remembered, and not to have lived and been understood?
I think to all the canyons gold and the rivers red to evenings glowing like stars in the desert, to the day extending past our own existence to fashion out of our own limbs others who shall never have listened to stories spoken in our skin—

(she spoke to me in a hologram of my dreams)

And perhaps people, images in light—all one and the same.

Cadence

The cadences upon the ground, spread to the desert earth cracked, and color draining from the sky.

Seeking youth as I grow old. How far to go backwards to search for that very first image of a garden cast in light?

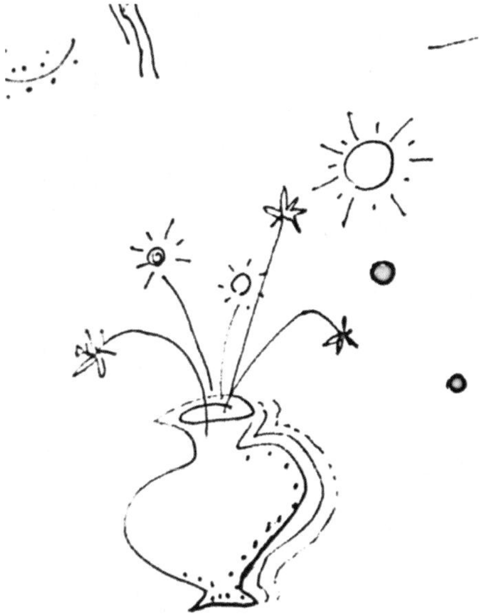

ABSTRACTIONS UNDER LIGHT

It was crespuscule, and only so…

It was crepuscule quand je suis arrivée. The air, the sound, the feel on the skin. It was like the loosening of arms, limbs after loving you, like the softly padded drumming of the timpani on parade as it walked away to another street, like the faded ink washes on the card that we folded up and sent to 36 linden. Or the way that hands meet and then separate as if sugar, caramelized, still connected them. But perhaps more so, the shadows of the sounds of footsteps, all blue and indigo and soundless, like silk screens—all dusk, and no dawn. Softly faded, the air smelled like clothes, freshly washed, hung out to dry before the rain; softly faded, j'essayais de m'échapper, but the intrusion came early. And suddenly, the light. As striking as the dark. It came, soundless, like the innards of a silent storm.

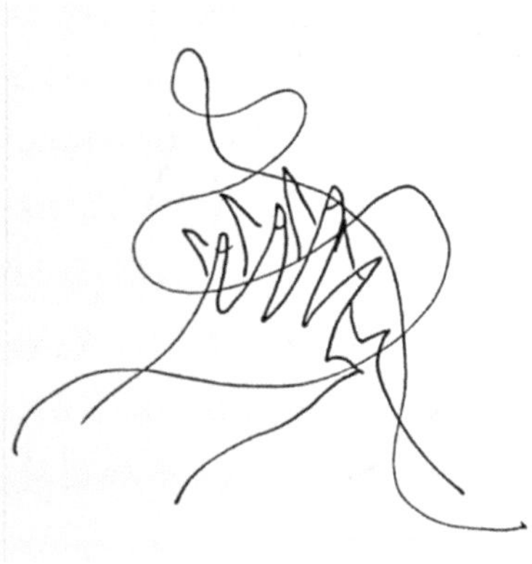

on the emphasis of shadows…
in the same way, i suppose, of all
that didn't seem to matter. the light
turned the other way, toward
a conversation i was not
listening to. inside the damp
corridor, the dark room,
shadows and the irregular
angles that they possessed
danced off the walls in rough
grayscale ecstasy. it was only
of light, but there were indeed
movements in light, and palpitations
of all things felt, and not
seen, and there were flutterings
in a nature akin to things like
"the roar of the absence of sound"
or the "blacked-out silhouettes
of discarded shapes." such was
their dance: eerie and ephemeral,
soft and angular, primitive yet
contained, as if echoes of the
shadows from a brushfire
in the Amazon. "one too many,
my dear," she had said.

To understand the stories
of shadows, one must understand
the palpitations from which
they are born: felt but not seen,
once feared, then discovered,
given to disappear, but not
to be understood—they are
a light all on their own;
and the girl, safe in the
palpitations of shadows in
an adjacent room, off of
a corridor in which a lamp
faced the other direction,
she too is a shadow, having
once been discarded by the light.

Dawn-avant shifting

Chill chilly chill tingling sounds breath-less breathing speaking softly as if a crime committed as intertwined we speak of sins a sudden shift slash of neon lights or the slash of shimmering skirts and nude lips softer and fleshier than a ripened peach half-melted on a summer's eve when last we spoke of stamp-shadows imprinted on skin and other softened substances the wafting of a cognac and smoke a sudden struggle a daggered-slipper and a camera clash foreshadows shards of glass like a strike of lightening it ends and softly softly it chills skin tingling sleeping I open an eye and I see enclosed in white everything encased in ivory and gold and glitter summertime seeds of grasses sifting and provençal sundrops like fireflies suspended and clean linen smells softening in sun on a string invisible and softening slowly slowly and all of a sudden I open an eye—

On | Off

It was the horror of having to see things so clearly, a glare of a lamp turned on not to illuminate but to transfix me as it shined past my consciousness and disengaged me from the freedom of the inward focus that I am almost always seeking in the sensation of evening wind going through cyclamens;

I switch it off.

And just like that, like the fireflies one sees inside after the eyes adjust slowly to a "darkness", so often filled with the subtle infinity of another nebula, so did my soul slowly switch on, lights sheer, and slowly gaining strength.

Slowly dilating space

Slowly dilating space so that objects far away grow in our feverish mind and suddenly burst open and objects once close disintegrate into a room dark or light and we cannot grasp at the walls for fear they are no longer standing still where they used to stand; rearranging shelves so that the old is easier to reach in our newly old limbs that stretch like cracked canvases in order for us to obtain the things at the start—so she says for us to imagine her, for she shall not exist if we do not imagine her; searching sound searching souls and so we search again among the acoustics scatter-contained in an amphitheater too solemn for the sun…

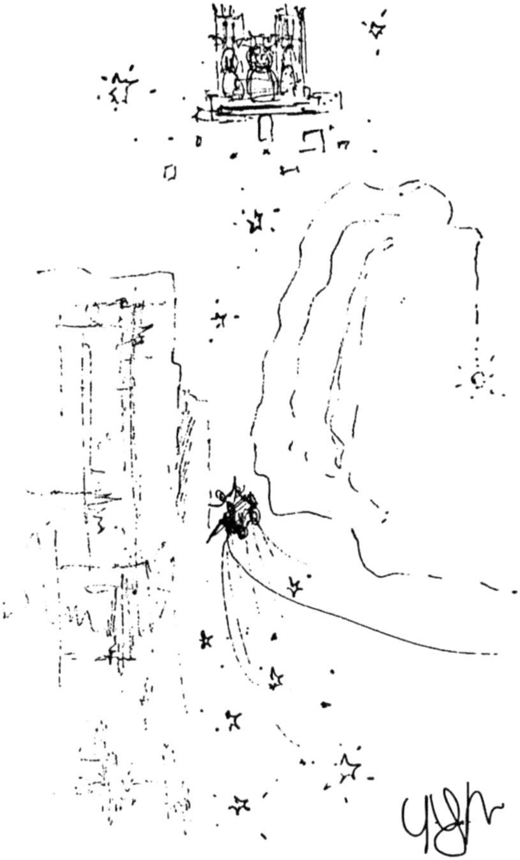

On Stars like Cathedrals

As the lights dimmed in sheer translucent silver dangling off a cliff and some sort of weak ecstasy we set out to discover everything in a red oxen cart up a rugged hillside that all at once reminded us of violets and rain and old men's beards showering sprinkles on us that tasted like coco memories and i, i closed my eyes gently as we swerved up a corner and felt the vibrations of bums laughing to the hilarious emptiness of an audience of sky and saw in the darkness stars like cathedrals oh yes! they were cathedrals because they hummed with the giant vastness of space that only cathedrals have on earth, and were solid like stone yet ethereal like the way cathedrals climb toward sky, and they twinkled something holy like the sweet voices of a children's choir, and as we left them I saw myself from a distance standing immovable with my face turned upwards but something was transporting away my soul; standing there in the dust-swirled road in a gallon hat and desperado i could hear the engines roaring on chasing the storm clouds as they loomed courting the shadows dancing in a strange primal relay along the distant mountainsides and as we fell asleep with a dream in our arms the one we bought at a dime at a corner stand in a street laced with lanterns along all the distant sidewalks—they are all shadows—and on Sundays even the devil has to go to church to study the soul sometimes.

Story of les pissenlits perdus

A stranger came in on Sunday morn, and as soon as -- sat down, began to speak,

"…so the snow found its way in through the gaps of my vulnerabilities, buried inside the folds of my coat, so it found me

exposed

where I thought I was wrapped up like she always said it would."

"…Bundled up I thought that I'd lie hidden, that my secrets would stay still, silent like Norma's eyes on Sunday morns when only the sparrow sings its idle song at the passersby; yet it had found me (lost me) as it came in stinging through the cracks—like the words of the preacher as they sought to unearth me, in places I'd kept solid for years…

The snow, it showed me but didn't teach or perhaps I simply couldn't comprehend: it was a lesson that, like love, believed in the principle that pain is a better stimulant than pleasure—so it came, cold and uninviting; it left me as an outsider looking in envious as to what could've been, reminiscing about what wasn't mine, lost in the streetlight where the snow coalesced like summer flies, without an aim in the lostwanderingworld except that of which to disarm me…until I saw, the pages of a book I'd been carrying loosely without care, its pages scattering wildly, as if they were ready to fly away at a moment's notice…

I realized standing there in the cold—exposed, bundled, confused, lost, idle—that the pieces of the book were like pieces of my soul: separate, it lacked a unifying theme but taken apart each had something in itself…as the breeze scattered them into far-off places I'd never see but perhaps saw once in eyes translucent with pain and memory, under the lamplight I stood until darkness-giving I could see them no longer…And they would never come back to me as a message from a peace-giving dove but instead they shall pass, shall pass from one hand to another from one heart to another until someday some bard will collect the pieces and string them all together some collectiveentity that someone will read some entitycollected that someone will love…

…but until then I wait here, as my scattered pages ils flottent dans le vent comme les échos des pissenlits perdus searching for a home in the soil where they'll grow, the smell of your dreams enticing me to stay in a subterranean jungle of angular light and from your thoughts to invent, a story of my own."

Gray intercession between sky and eyes

And what else to be, but infinitely close,

in the gray intercession between sky and eyes?

In the skewn-skewed stick silhouettes black as tar and hard as stricken celestial ash, in the interspace between sky and eyes stories too strange to tell and too far away to reach but only to behold, just like your fingers intertwined in mine only to sin what else is there to do? on the journey to speed, vitesse, ssta-ccato smooth ebony there is a story pounding pounding underneath us trying to let go, lift back your neck fly back your arms feel infinitesimally small and feel alive as it reverberates through and under carrying us to the endless stretch of destiny etched of light in darkness and see the way the light starts not as a glimmer but as a shield that only lets in; oh let us live scarlet ochre sienna songs of the desert gleaming, hungry and glorious, silent and beating in its coldness—

and in the evening, come close to me, infinitesimally close to me, i am cold, but do not come close enough skin not even touching can you feel me close infinitely close like a rose like a rose faint smell do you feel it reverberating through and inside of you? come close to the fire but do not let it singe you like it singed me once and you fell asleep arms still around me as i lay awake eyes open to the storm to the endless silent storm a dancer in the gray intercession between sky and eyes and your breathing constant and heavy arms around me as i lay awake and counted the stars that couldn't ever grow up and die away but lay frozen like fetuses; sunlight shadows clocking the day as it grows across the desert cactus statues and grasses swimming in a garden of Eden dryer than a prostitute's soul can it be saved? sell our soul as one, on the road again the lines flying back alive like a code we are fine to throw away and forget and leave in the dust again and again;

Do you feel the pounding the pounding it reverberates through and under us carrying us to a destiny etched in light of darkness, to feel the way we feel close and infinitely close, skin not even touching can you test your limits see the cactus flowers flaming under testimony of the stars see—

Stepping at once into darkness, stepping at once into light.

Sunstreaking through the pillars on the north side of Frist campus center creating shadow pillars on the ground. Walking through, shadow pillars erected invisible. Curtains of another dawn, or a fast-speed railway in a tunnel of yesterday's confusion. The uncertainty and delicious of danger, light and darkness juxtaposed, in sequence certain in uncertainty. To overcome your fear among the shadows is something to be forgotten, just like the way the daisy bloomed in the flowerpot, unnoticed, and left Tuesday afternoon.

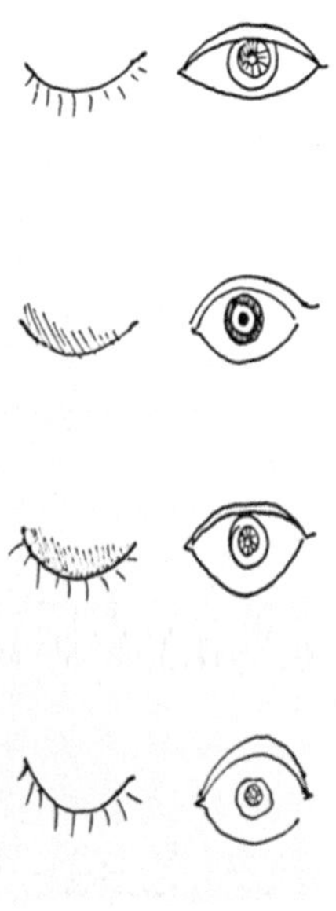

We drove by that stop once without stopping, ghosts of places past, like the fence on the edges of mon esprit. Eyes peeking through pine boards, not quite knowing what to see, not being able to see, not seeing. If perhaps I closed my eyes, I could see better in the darkness, but what truth could that bring, unless truth does not consist of light? But in darkness, truth does not quite belong either. Anything can happen—even the imagined have their own costumes, *somersaulting like tainted angles dressed in caramelized plastic suits in a tunnel where perhaps he lies waiting for me to come.* It is strange, standing between or across or I don't know, stranded in-between two extremes of light and other-light, and in Suzhou I am crying from a doorway into the sun…or like the way this pensée is stranded across the page. It is cut-off like severed heads that do not think about seeking their other part…don't you see? It gnaws at the stump of soul you have left, sifts the heterogeneous sand in your veins back and forth like some strange sandfilled hourglass that switches between gravities…closes one eyelid in exhaustion and opens another in surprise. Contrast is powerful, always, because it renders us uncomfortable.

I am always scared. Always stranded in-between the two bridges I have yet to cross. The feet are cold, the arms are burning. If only they, among other things (like minds and hearts, nightmares and dreams, youth and old age) were connected to each other to soften the contrast, to filter the blood and lessen the fall. Always scared that tomorrow the sun comes around a different side, and I will no longer be stranded between two bridges, one of darkness and one of light (but only one of darkness, you see?).

Somewhere, somewhere, lost in the ainoma of places, the ghosts pass through my eyes (once gorgeous in the light). And I am standing suspended at the gate, suspended without latch or shadow.

In the linden forest, caught in shards of the late afternoon sun, ink-somber steles chanting solemnly.

Chasing ombres

Chaa-sing ombres—chaa-sing shadows
L'âme se promène au-dessus de mon corps,
The soul strolls above my body.
Past la colline and where the soldiers go,

And the streets, they were named after saints.

She liked the feeling that it gave her. That cold gray, yellowing sort of sun, one that came late in the afternoon before the sun-set-slept after a day of raining that exhausted one's steps, of the sort that as it shined through the only non-shaded window adjacent to her cubby in the recess of the study library feebly a cause de its physical strength but sturdily a cause de its spirit, the fenêtre speckled with dirt and grime and other caked delights, residue of silences left unspoken, it came in and stopped short and didn't fill the seeking room but instead chose to fill her eyes—sockets and all—

and in her face it stood and smiled and left her suspended without need of support or another desk to lean on, *only light only light*, like a pair of lover's eyes that collapses you from within but also suspends you, incredible immovable standing strength; *only light*, and after it subsided, slow steps and wandering eyes and a song of swirling leaves, down below and up above, as it should be. cold. autumn. day.

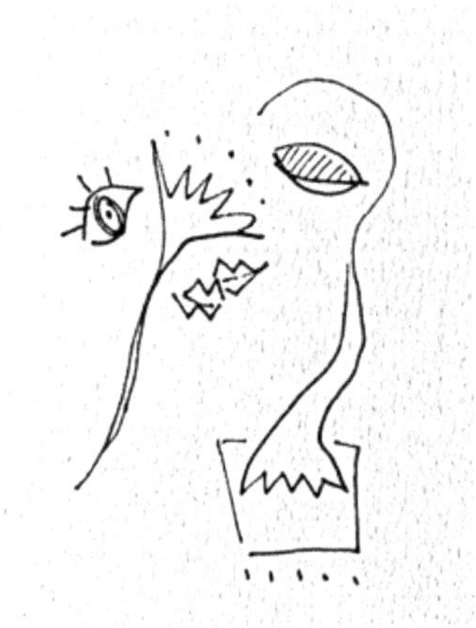

On the radio, she cried and she crooned and she sighed that she'd rather
go blind, than yes, to see you walk again, so we close our eyes...

..fternath of a candle

She said she'd rather go blind than to see you walk again so we close our eyes and let the long shadows fall on our eyelids and let the rich warmness of the coffee stains intoxicate the autumn leaves the smells of musk leaving a wet imprint that sticks to skin, clothes, and equally our encyclopedia of imaginings, mahogany batik on ivory concrete like mother's bread with rubies of cranberries leaving an impression, scattered… someone told me once that the rain is desensitizing, sanitizing, clears away the debris of autumn crisps of souls shipwrecked upon the sidewalk, stuck in-between cracks like the sesame seeds that fell curiously, purposefully,

inconsiderately, from the beggar's sesame cookie into the cracks of the old wooden table in the garden overrun by man's neglection and recently-discovered freedom; so child, let the rains come! let it scatter away and cleanse us of our sorrows engraved into the cracks that one day shall form the wrinkles of our soul, carry them away like a stream in ecstasy and plant them in fields where they can grow to our advantage, create soil that tastes sweet like foggy dews of childhood, bitter like old age and hickory-smoked could-a-done's, gritty like surprises, rich like a love that leaves you without object but with itself and everything to remember her by, so it is in that garden I had imagined we once sat, beneath the shutters of a window reflected of that summer sky inflamed, clouds softly folding into leftover tea sitting bathing in its own residual warmness; the two little china cups, delicate although they thought themselves strong, on the wicker table somewhere lost, as she leaves sans adieu, like the flicker of a candle quivering on a promise built on uncertainty…it is reflected in the street window all the lamplights and all the cars, and we saw in the soft illumination of the café where safety in comfort sleeps, a silhouette in the sun whose face we cannot see;

In that summer we had climbed the fence to the other side and saw the sun as it fell or perhaps came up, speeding into the distance—once again going forward to arrive at le commencement…

Softly she cried, it was all over, all over. And on her closed eyelids, the long shadows extended and imprinted an image of the slow wick of the candlestick—once again the image, but not the object itself.

Solemn laughter echoing in green, orchard-shaded soliloquy the movement of cars as camouflage for sin and what shade eerily catches of lolita's song la tendresse of unripened fruit or overripened desire the sweetest fruit under the sun;

still, we didn't know of the ailment or the cure. she lay in bed sick for months immovable. it wasn't thirst, although she was parched, no amount of rain or the sounds of rain could arouse her, and it wasn't memory, or the lack of, but perhaps it had all been invention. her steps clattered up the stairs, my own solemn steps muted in lead didn't attempt to chase hers. today i let her go i l e t h e r g o and escape me; i couldn't catch her anymore if I tried.

curiously, two shadows encased in silver caught in the cold of a valley encased in snow. a little tingly-sly comforting rire. frozen were we, not in snow but in time soul time which may have been just a figment of a light, a flame struck inside an igloo—the image of which I can quizás also capture in a shoebox…it dissolves like a dandelion, shaped like the sun but shimmers in silver, a thousand little dispersions of insanity.

Could I sew your shadow? could I still imagine our song and the way we danced like summer silhouettes swinging chandeliers of chardonnay and storms, the way you had left a sweet trail of fingertip ignition in the AM on the tips of the invisible hairs on my stomach before we too ignited like silken suns? quite a sad little laugh it is; clothed and all. it couldn't dance naked under the stars the way it had once in Eden. it stormed. stars smiled at us before we slept, summer stars but not in the thick underbrush of carnal inhibition in the dark greens of oils on a canvas where no light could pass; so I slept, and solemnly the stars stopped smiling as she cried, soft inhibited tears that tried for a chance at mañana but only stopped short of the current. i stood still. I could see she was still smiling, dangling apples from los arboles in the garden shimmering with sounds of that smile…i stood still. In the silence of the cathedral i glanced up, and her same smile came up in simplistic ignorance of all that is left, of all that had left and is gone.

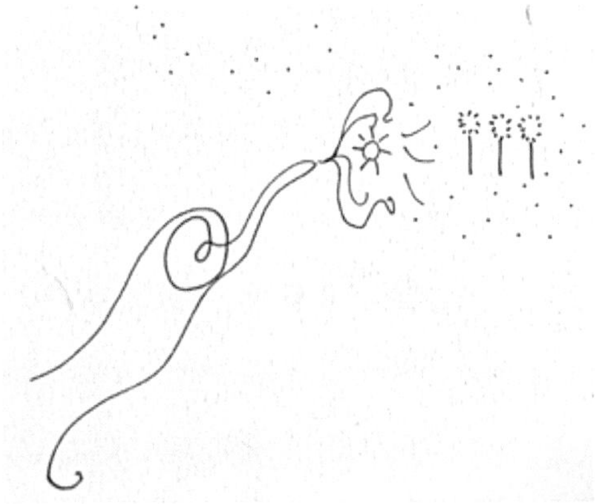

As if
the answers
lay among and between the sheets
scars and emblems
of everything that could—
two kids cutting their own path between yesterday's leaves and tomorrow's
emptiness,
as if
the answer
could even be found, could even
lie
in echo of

the truths of the barren lands,
now filled with snow—
flesh and fire,
and the erosion of the Image
that burns alive in destruction—
the taste is only bitter
as in the color gray.

After everything is over
in the aftermath of longing
only a shadow-lingering-shadow
on the sidewalk where used to walk
many moons
and many dawns

leaving their
footprints
like stamps
a c r o s s t h e s a n d like longings unfulfilled
and yet unblemished.
All we have left
is left
in the ferments
of our imagination—
once pure,
once undisturbed
once olvidan and forgotten
like the storm-reflected pond

standing still—

soiled-footprints of that year's
song, still traveling south:
fernweh not for places unknown
but for places lost
and such skies olvidan
seeking always
a dawn imprinted.

Those who walk away

The same, the samba, and the darkness of the crowds. All going somewhere. And those who walk away, but only some to come back of their own accord.

Couldn't be so sure

So I found myself in the same spot that someone else had once been sitting in. In the dark, in a dragon's cave, eyes piercing into the light, except this time she had been looking in. As if she could see me even as I was losing myself into the abyss.

Confusion. Transgression. Transcendence. Transfiguration. Translation.

As I saw her body disjointed with her dreadlocks and her shape, as I saw him transgress into her hands, smooth with polish, scarlet as an oiled lip glossy and dangerous—it could only be a woman's hands, but I couldn't be so sure. One cannot be too sure.

Slowly, translation, as I felt my body sinking into my own hands. Conscious, of what they could and couldn't do. As my fingers danced their strange primal dance underneath the lamplight. As they sought life, and slowly, yet ever increasingly slyly, sought a way out from the rest of me that stayed behind in the subtleties of an inner cavern—and all that is left unexplored. Unexposed, and somewhere our greatest secret: warm, dark, and moist. The beginning is our end, and the end is our beginning—caught beneath the attic light.

Orphic

I shall always remember them caught in light one side of her face smiling or rather caught in scattered gold the way I imagined Eurydice to look as she was coming up and not the way she would return Such a gold it was! for it was so golden so yellow but not yellow so rich but so sharp and scintillating yet deep and unspoken so emanating so enveloping and projecting out as I'll never see again such a gold as Orpheus would've liked to see but couldn't yet here I was sideways on a sidewalk | side-walking sideways and I could glimpse into the eternity that only chance could offer her smile and that goldenness in angular form before it scattered into gray into the disillusionment of smoke She was gold but the cavern was gray so were the shadows and the chalk left on the walls scribbles of love or the promises of eternity of the innocence that comes with the excitement of the incertitude and not of the corruption that comes with the acceptance of the same Yes that was what it was but for now it is what it is only shadows peeling off the walls in confused uncertainty as I calmly stretched out my hands to collect them as they fell one by one into the tunnel so uncertain in its gray-gold gold-gray equivocal oscillation and I'll be here to catch them if they slide and fall upon the ice reflecting all their gold blinding them in all their eyes as they cross the lake on the day when the fishes sleep but there is time to grow and time to be yellow and now they are but two two shadows slow-drifting away into the tunnel scattering into smoke…

Light abstractions

Even as the day absorbs into evening, eyeing the clouds as they churn in speeds of paranoia, pink rimmed as they speckle into lamplight, as the twisted iron sculptures of giacomettian trees melt into the stone, as car headlights blink on and blink off like a juror in the almost-darkness, illuminating one's underexposed dreams in the soft belly of a yet limitless silence—in this safe haven, we are unaware, as the world inside churns to become one with the one outside, a momentary flurry of confusion, between what is light and what is dark, and what is lighter still;

Abstractions arise. Smooth motion has arisen, starting and ending like a comma suspended on an endless string, crossing the bridge like a lunar vein, speeding and continuing along the balconies of another universe suspended;

little eyes in the night searching for mary among the rhododendron leaves and the leaves upon the shelves, as we glance up to stars golden like two hundred suns who forgot where they belonged, in silent confusion as we glance up and look and pray, and see that it is only a ceiling, for we are free to imagine,

as the ceiling becomes sky and sky becomes ravaged ceiling, as woman becomes part man and man becomes part woman, as the sea sings-lies as the sailor lies shipwrecked, caring never to return, to spend that momentary voucher, to live a life sans separation or definition or obstruction;

So it is, to become one with the rain as he touches the sun, to see the light as the darkness closes in upon him; yet it is only the darkness, and not the light that chooses him, self-stifilation of schrodinger's oscillation, as the swings stop swaying in sudden impulse in anticipation of the silent storm, and those who stayed behind to see the light see what it is really—fifty orbs in phosphorescent glow on the ceiling, orbs that could've been strange stars by lucid lamplight, and dreams caught by paranoia now only dreams by ink imprinted, the cabinets and shelves with pages suspended, no bridge of starry sighs or calcite crystal but only stairs of wood and iron, not a duality but always the separation, and as we look outside from within, this time, only a dim dim reflection of ourselves.

Little I ’ chapel

It’s the intangible see-through soleil and ombre of sidewalk chalk swinging like shadows on and along the old walls that stay constant through sun and after-sun and oversun a song of blue and yellow of houses and ochre of roofs and warm warm sienna and the strange sea green of van gogh and cézanne over olive like in derain’s pinéde à cassis that shocks me and I close my eyes to the distant coldness of a chapel dressed in its finest white cold serenity in a closed space yet so limitless its soundless bells singing in the valley below echoing in silver and in shades of periwinkle twinkling dangling from la mystère and la moustier-re-de-sainte-marie…
sitting all alone little I ’ chapel what are you thinking about, sitting alone on your summit snudged in between a statue and the wing of a prayer in your strange heaven so far above us all? yet it is not quite close enough to be in a heaven of your own with the skies so far above you too so she stays solitude in solidity stoic and eyes soft somewhere it’s the variations of dark chords resting on a blue stage like the vibrations felt after a storm searching for something I once thought I had too yet only as intangible as the ombre of the storm, in staccato or in constancy, in lightning or in smoke, and I caught myself imagining once again—mais il est interdit, il est interdit…

As in the drops left
in-between the crevices;
caught in the cracks
of sea and storm and the
violet passage
of time—to erase what had
been is not the same, just
like the way
evening looks
under lamplight. She danced a
dance, they said, filled with
a fire (creamy and
opaque and lost in time) filled with the sharp irregular silhouettes of
the confusion
(and only the confusion) of desire,
fury desire, and
the sweet-sour deep a-ro-ma
of angular past moments—
So it is, as they slowly
scuttle along back to sea, as I
look
to the long stretch of the
crisp blue solitude
that flickers and flames
smoke dancing fire
on the thin blue line of my life,

as the ships
draw away like little stick figures
of the Spanish toys I had
once
or a thought unchained
left unspoken
(shadows adding depth
to this saying unsaid)
fluidity of an ethereal liquid
behind solid screens of my sunken lids—only
slowly do they return
uncertain
as if, their ideas could leave their footprints and change the landscape forever
as if, forgiveness was a virtue—
Slowly they crinch back
uncertain but with cer-tain-ty,
slow beat commanding
of the *aveugle's* s i g h t
in darkness.

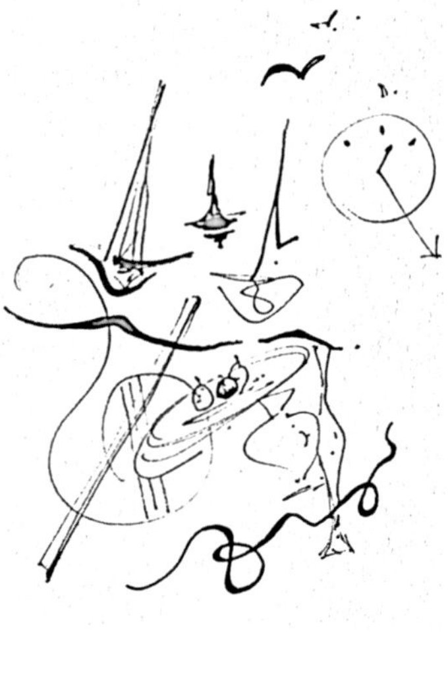

game of deception

She's standing at the second-from-left upstairs window, alone. The soft light from the hallway outside the room behind her lights up a few strands of her hair, the ones called flyaways that need to be cut; light also illuminates the soft silhouette of her back, her face yet dark to the evening.

Nothing in particular—she said. And it was true.

It is difficult to tell, if she meant that she had seen it before, or if it had appeared for the first time, and the first time only. Yet to her, everything was always new, scented with the beauty and the magnificence that comes with time past, even if it had all once been a game of deception.

On the streets, children play, candles flickering, voices trailing off like a chorus into the distance.

The steeple sleeps

A drop fell down from the tree and disappeared on the asphalt. The ghosts of cars drive by through the light of hollowed-out places—wherever you looked there were friends or ghosts of where they used to stand, puddles beneath the sunlight.

And at noon in the village, the sun is out and all is quiet.

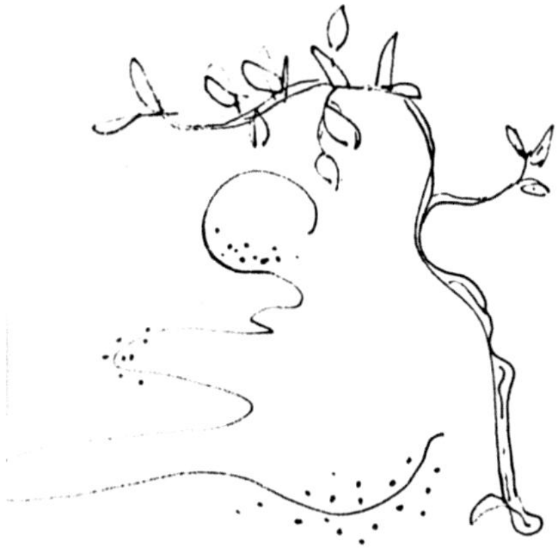

IMAGES IMPRINTED

Invisible

In the city formless, there is no grid; every time you go outside, in the singular muddle only pods of existence if you search hard enough, corners of churches and street-stands where they gather in cauliflower heads and blank black-moor stares—there is no one to ask where we are going, no one to ask to what we belong…little colonies of crab-children, seeking a place deep in the quiet of sand among the seaweed skyscrapers, is there a place where you can lie down for a second, lie down and go to sleep? and tomorrow a place where you can swim up and see the sky qui vaut la peine of all those stories? It is only up to us to ask where we are going, to ask for what we are living for, lost in these seawater colonies of blue-gone souls in these corners of blue-gone dreams…For in the emerald city invincible, we are but invisible.

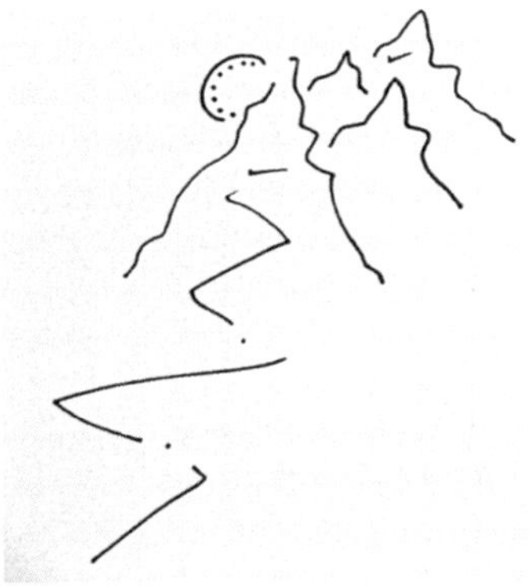

I felt as if I were walking the streets at 1am in the morning laughing at the hollow sky specked with liquid stars and the image of the desert wild and white as moonlight and the way it seemed to stretch out like somebody's fingers, slender continuity in such ghostly alabaster stone. I saw us speeding into the darkness along a continuous road, and somewhere in the wild hazy dusk of it all I could still feel the shadows of yesterday's origami mountains looming in the distance—blue and gray and the haze of evening violet the colors of shadows upon the translucent coral of inverse dawn such skyscrapers in the city the way they too seemed 2D and pasted like paper cut-outs of transparent matissian style onto the great open expanse of lonely-desert-sky, sky gray as a drunk and pure as a virgin, and all of it—the desert, the ghosts, the origami mountains—all filled me with such blues, and the only thought I could formulate in my head I mumbled over and over again: if talking to mountains could substitute talking to rivers…

I started to feel like I was folding into and onto myself, continuously, like gradually falling into a deep deep well that had no bottom yet I was folding folding just like a thick piece of cotton paper folding and I could easily lose myself this way—if only I could just let go of thinking and trying so hard to "be"—but I was scared to, scared of the thought of eternity…and I was much too awake; so I did everything I could from folding in further;

finding myself again, perhaps losing myself forever.

Cigarette smoke

Straining to stay awake, as I am, projected infinite onto images drenched in dark dimezone of liquid allusions that lead to nothing, I stare into the image of another face another name of another skinny flat-chested girl with eyes like stories and hair tangled up in smoke;

I stare into the silver of a lake with no reflection.

So sing the sins that speak—shimmering lights that perspire in the cold—under the lamplight and above the sinews of the cigarette smoke from the bystander who waited there, drifting upwards drenched and heavy, waiting too for something after rain;

I exhale to a cloud with no direction.

Where oh where is the tunnel with the shadow of the man leading into light? Skipping stones on the cobblestone as the invisible feet of the invasion of dreams escape unnoticed; through the village and under your window overlooking the street, and here I am asking the question to the choir of the simple red glare of uncertainty: how can I escape from the fire | escape left unopened? but digressions of this sort lead to long skinny fingers climbing up the cord,

like yellow…
like yellow…

But no yellow butterflies. Suddenly the strange certainty of your arm around and over my chest as you lie sleeping, and I am empty and gone, even as the extension cords slowly exhaust what little I had left and leaves my fingers tingling, tied up like pincers on helium balloons and losing circulation, even as they are undone slowly, like a balloon half-submerged that never leaves anchor.

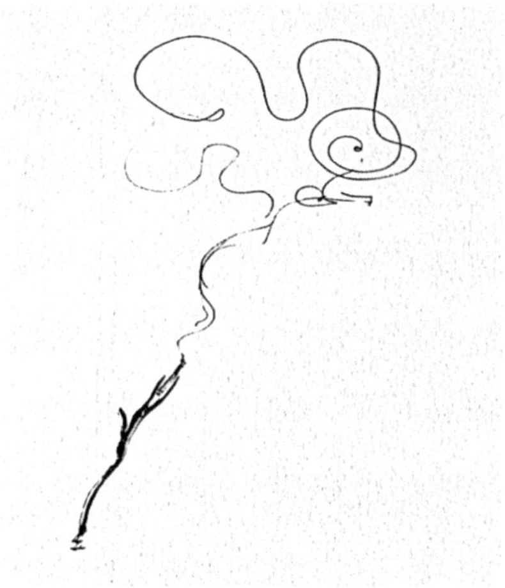

Broken shadow children

All the broken shadow children of the earth who seek some kind of redemption emerge along dirt highways and ten dollar motels and Indian summer nights in the fields ripe with hay and emanating with the sweet musty fragrance of pubescent desire swarming with junebugs lighting everything with innocent fire and soon the whizz of all the characters going by, the Deans and Marylous of the earth, singing a sad sad song full of an unquenchable longing although it is never one of regret—I ask what is it they seek (the pearl at the end of the journey?) and what is it that we are trying to prove, beneath the giant blue vault of the sky laced with tears and dreams and eyes withered by looking out forever to a distant sunshine nonexistent here but perhaps perhaps elsewhere—

only sometimes do I even dare to feel their pain but usually I just envy them I envy them for their longings and especially for their freedom and cannot help but see it clearly, picking cotton in the field fingers raw and bleeding and kneeling down in a prayer on the soft earth and in the evenings return to a lover in my arms and especially especially the freedom to not care to not care about anything or anybody and to feel fine about leaving anyone at will god that'd be a thousand times swell don't you think? no strings to attach me back to the things toward which I have feelings to the heart where I have roots (oh gracias don Pablo!) knowing that I've been long long gone rising and billowing in my solo balloon raving in the clouds overflowing in exuberant excitement not knowing or caring which way to go and continuously, the pieces are falling back swirling down to earth rendering me penniless…but perhaps someday, losing everything, I can finally feel free to try, anything.

’espace entre indigo

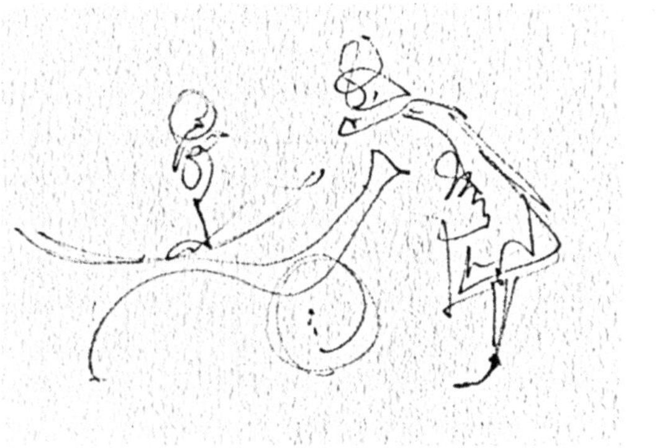

The space between indigo is where you’ll find me, curled up between layers of grandma’s calico quilt, two bridges to and from childhood fantasies tissue-box castles and things and i still sophie doll’s hair entangled in clips that swam in a sea of goldfish by the stained-glass window jars that caught the sun until they became so filled with sun they slowly lost their colors, but only on the outside; so it’s simplicity dried like mangos in a plastic bag sealed in the trunk saved for eating later, salt and pepper shake, and all other things delectable like the imagined vapors steaming from the kitchen de la poupée on a summer porch seven inches long. If you could see, if you could see, if you could take off your shoes and paint in the foam like a brush just wet enough and dry enough, improvisation at its finest until the tide comes in, if we could lose ourselves in the reeds or in the grasses in the prairie and drink the silences of the stars and wrap ourselves in the vast lamentable space that is the intercession between eyes and sky, and sky and heart, and the age and years of all things past and come again, as she stood there, dressed in so many dresses of white unpolluted by the stains in the grasses green, sleeping under the stars it was, cleaner than the sky with its infinite sorrows, an effect upon the years cleaner than coal in its infinite oblivion.

Ce qui me sauve

It is to see your image in a mirror un-focalisé avec la dust qui se trouve plus importante as we climb the ropes that singe our skin seeking the path to the golden-yellow bridge to yesterday's light, somewhere in the green…somewhere lost and somewhere found the deep golden hues of green and gargoyle envisionings there is a bowl to keep the discrepancies from alighting like a phoenix does in fire, so memory often plays tricks on us but reality always wins the game, and little did we know memory was only on our side and reality was the one who was always laughing like the way time laughs at old age, so we struggle to keep inborn such desires of our inflaming spirit and it is easier in cathedral quiet sheltered between the dank solemnity of moist moss that silently suffocates and of our ghosts and internal devils what left temporarily loozes and likewise soozes the dryness of trees so I find myself digressing, from the original path or starting point that the huntsman put me on in order to allow me to escape, "continue forward," he said, "and never look back until you've burned your bridges" so why did I, go backwards instead of forwards, choose to cross once again the bridges, choose the traveled path instead of the safer unknown?—the only difference is this path is my own and only my own, they forget that once you burn the bridge the smoke gets in your eyes, and il faut que je croie that our past is not a cage it sets you apart from the others it sets you free.

Space in-between once we stepped out into the cold. Stood, looked up, and questioned.

Everywhere reflected—silence and the image of stars, creativity in the absence of starlight; one must remember it was only autumn and the snows had not yet come. Outside on the string invisible, snowflakes a-fresh suspended a question inside of me, like stardust that awakens a mound of heaviest silence and scatters them in silver. Scattered like cold orgastic circulation, sprinkles of snow fire ash or the origins of something. Individually contained, yet letting go. Suspended somewhere; frost.

My soul, now lanterns. suspended silver in the cradles of eve. Earlier I was so small, stumbling I closed my eyes, everything contained but still caught crying—sky feeling sorry it hung me up to dry on silver lines invisible. There is space in suspension like there is space in openness; lost in circulation I couldn't feel small I could stay safe in such a paradox of shelter of our innermost organ, of nothing contained but the soul everywhere reflected and scattered, in the smallest seeds of silver. So it was I stayed to go and so the soul stays: open, and still suspended. Such is this stardust on a string, and one day I shall look for it again, such strange substance as containing and letting go, of

souls, streets, stars.

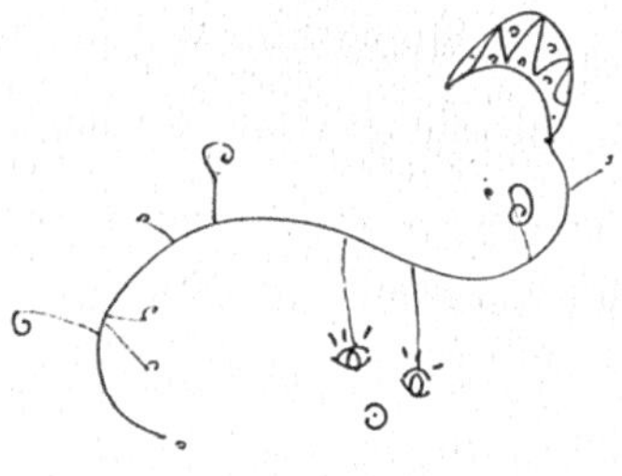

The Sculptor

It started with “it seems like nothing ever lasts” and suddenly, grew too old for me to catch, submerged underwater, only a set of piercing eyes back in the studio where it all began, stone face fixation slowly cracking au-dessus et en dessous skin,

to the sculptor’s dismay, on the day when he had come to sculpt he finds she had once been broken, and of course interior cracks are the ones hardest to fix and it was

hidden from view from all but you and now only the clouds that are faded gray, stirring up in split view a stormy sky and a pine tree in confused stoic solemnity, trust and distrust slowly synonymous, even as the clouds are falling like raindrops on skin, fading fading away; just like the sculptor’s hands as they slowly caress the object he loved before forgetting, so had Pygmalion forgotten her, little flower on fire encased in stone her cold marble curves defiant in their weak ashen fragility that smiled and forgave but could refute no longer, such incroyance of sailors’ returns once they embark in search of the sea;

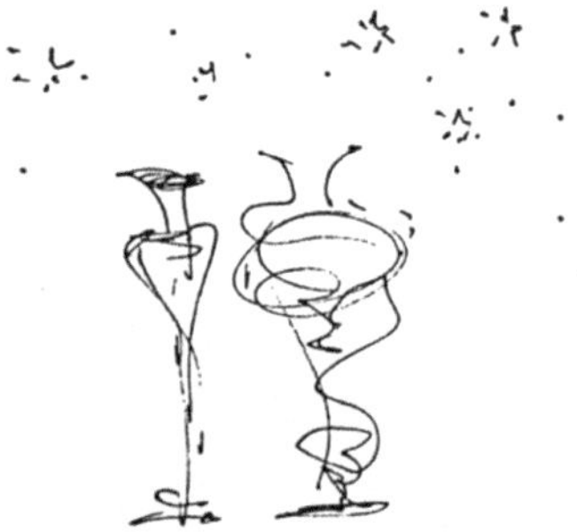

so the light glossed over and above the sidewalk of our childhood, not really searching, just a little flashlight in the cave where we used to play, imagine-searching for originals of aborigines; it was, just an empty street of garbage-leaves, little autumn specks asking for footprints or forgiveness—only where have they all gone? Only shadows reflected in eerie Pompeian certainty something or other of you and something or other of me, but our story was real and so were the footsteps stones that shone gold in the agora-plane; our shadows the only sign we had existed. And so we knew, no more breaths and no more chords, collapsed and interlocked as one, the ephemeral solidity of the eternal weight of our contentful exhaustion—two shadows encased in stone as if we had indeed, once fallen from the stars.

Shadow-searching

Shadows, like stars, fall from trees like leaves, le bleu hiver and the motion of one's hand brushing it away; the little silver boats flashing and it is no longer a question of vision but a question of imagination; erasing the path to the outlawed land, it was as we once knew—easy and predictable—but if asked where it began, we couldn't say. The cave holds the answers that we seek (painted like the sun is, carved by tears and carved by stone, lying idle to anticipation), but always, the intruders—a liquid storm, death by light, and a shuffling fear of losing what we once had but gone again, and the unexpected saviours coming from a dark and seeping into our consciousness.

…Shadows, like stars, fall onto leaves like pieces of broken glass yet both hands outstretched to catch the stardust as it falls—ignites—like a thousand perfect storms on an otherwise perfect halcyon day, and it was as we sat on rooftops blushing at the dawn sipping away tomorrow as we sat blinking trying to preserve today clueless to a soundless guitar drumming us away to a fable of imagination a picture of a castle of lore that didn't even exist yet they are the only things that make us feel safe as we circle between truth and story,

even as story has no end
and truth has no beginning.

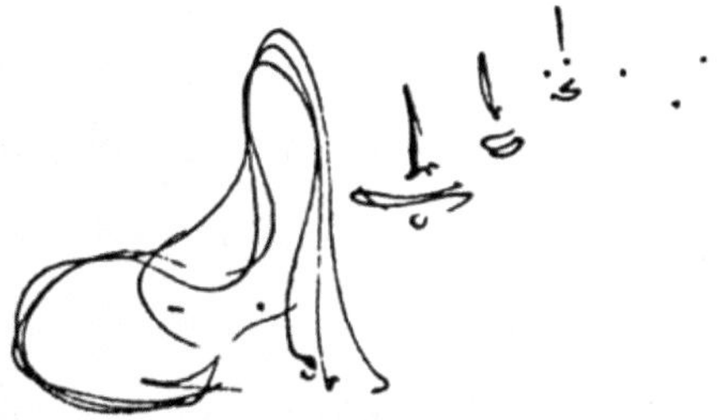

Dancer

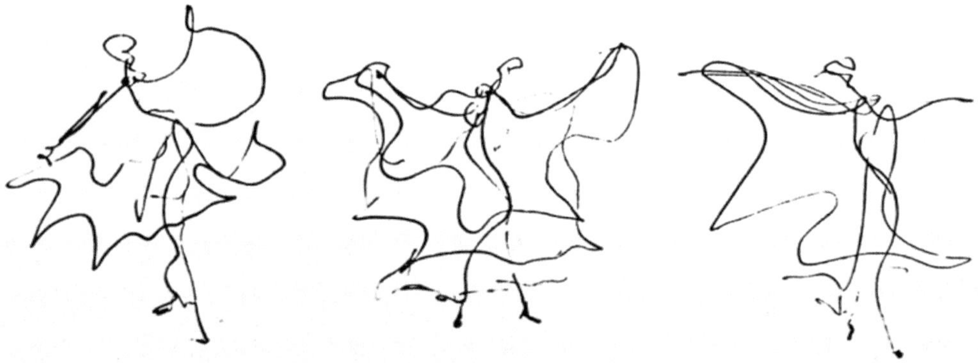

She is gorgeous. soft caramel sweater the color of her skin. unanimous. soft. sweet. on the corners of her sleeves I see seas and ships. there are little flounces. delicate and cream. not sharp white like folds. only creases in cream. in Seville, the roundness of sidewalk flamenco dances. only a time-passing sonic-disrupting it's-okay sort of glance since we are here and there are no spaces for sidewalks only sliding across linoleum and space enough for some other smile. seas and ships. cream and skin.

contrasting the fire, the thin white lace of the Veracruz dancers like intransient wings, symbolized a fluttering of circles a movement of arms a quality ungraspable almost invisible, shimmerings closest to the scent of lilacs, calling into mind what of proustian invisible lilacs, as they graced the air but left only a scent that speaks.

Little solitary dancer
Up a solitary slope of a mountainside;
Little dancer, dance
Yes little Izu dancer
Dance your pure emotion
Of softened veil and powdered eyes.

Little gypsy girl

Dry rain evaporates onto rich earth molten as the heat erupts like envelopes of smoke that lift and escape with a hiss, some volcanic eruption releasing perfumed packets smelling of oak and lavender, a hiss and aw ay like the train s w ay and stories its pages soaked by rain; somber chiffon ribbons of sorrow and dewy musk coated in autofiction nostalgia, like violet maroon with a hint of golden-gray, as they trespass across, intertwining...

And there was a little gypsy girl, one I lost in that white-blue city on a plateau that spring, in a café in plaka-laka where they had come to sing; children all and she alone with her liquid molten gray-green eyes staring at you with a hiss and something in you lifts and escapes like smoke; lovely tan beautiful girl with skin like earth, plaka-laka in the middle of the day in the center of the square in that well-established European café with its patrons in linens and other fabrics made of the fine quality of their afternoon teas and here these children had come, one with dirty hands one with too-big shoes one with dark-matted hair and the youngest with an accordion that he was still too shy to play, and they were a sad bunch all of them as people turned down their faces to turn back to the Greece that they had come to seek and not the one that came uninvited to seek them, all that was left in a bowl of horiatiki and yiaourti me meli and iced frappé, and of course the beautiful girl with skin like earth came last, sought eyes that sought hers and stood next to me, eyes searching inside of me for something I could not give, no, not in drachmas or pride or childish shame, and in that beautiful clean blue-white city well-lit by sun in all its places and cafés, there will be a day when just a little corner of one street will be soaked by rain, violent maroon with a hint of emerald smoke in that spot where she had stood, so naked, next to us—and she was only thirteen, but I had wondered what those eyes had already seen, had already heard in those alleyways where the sound of the accordion leaves not even an echo to claim.

. . .

lilacs shaped by—
invisible lilacs shaped by—
invisible charred lilacs—

on the ground.

An autumn later and we are wearing our long suede boots the same ones nana got us as a college gift and dark deep sunglasses stepping out of the car

to survey what had changed expecting it to stay the same—under the bridge, under the lights, and the dried crackled bushes outside the wooden taverns and shops in schoen's place as they did once in swann's way, only to see that it was empty, just like every other place devoid of leaves...
crackled and shriveled, they constituted what cold remembrances I still had of charred autumn leaves bathed in fire, embellishments not lacking, of coronated red and Sicilian orange lost in time. Aside. A lilac tree who in its emptiness stood, invisible lilacs to charred lilacs, somehow forgotten by the chimney smoke; a visible shadow of an invisible sound. It stood. Swept away, it still lingered. Charred deep purple to cake crackled cold of empty soil.

And Joey of the long hair and long limbs and shadowy but not unkind eyes was working at the little faux-Greek restaurant at the bottom of the basin where I had once eaten gyros and pronounced it wrong. I see him clearly, as he steps out in an apron in an abashed smile as he bends over to take out the trash to put into Thursday's bin, un-forgetting me in the process of forgetting. How strange time is. How invisible charred like leaves it seems.

A crash an interruption a heat wave torpedo the coldness of a colorblind September song in the sinews of an unforgiving voice reminding you of all existent and nonexistent flaws; looking back it's all the same.

How does one step back into things?

o much simpler

as the skin draws numb
like stars running off the page
little indescribable blue thoughts
erupting into ashes that
fall into the sea
as confusion
as hangliders peruse the valley
as the silver snakes stretch
shimmering scales shivering like silent sobs
and the dust draws into dawn
so she | I sits by the desk facing the
oblisque staring out to the eternity of
made-up words and seeing the sunrise
for the first time, as if in a land
foreign to that of one's native land
so close and so far away
to that first dream of antiquity
that started the stone wheel of
monotony, but it had seemed much
more colorful then,
and so much simpler,
until the forced fire cracked its
surface and shaped its structure to
an image of itself.

I couldn't really explain it, the coinciding of convulsions & convolutions, spheres going round and round again in concentric circles, single filing into eccentric circles. Searching for another life within another circle, surpassing another limit of our minds like the way we skip across subway doors into another car, arriving at another station, beyond ordinary the realms of our daily existence. It was the repetition of the unseen, but it was up to your own opinion if the unseen was the unsensed. Because in the air, there is always a sense of the sounds of the remnants of the unheard, if there was indeed such a thing. It was the space, stranged-strangled-and-stilled, of the space between storms, circles that powered the air with their perfumes of gray, smoke-heather, and slices of scarlet crimson. Invisible, of course, but whirling like fans caught in fantastic obligations on summers' eves when the last of the imaginations has been swept away of the one last gone and images completed, circling like the wheels of a train on the iron tracks chugging along as we rush to search for the something we left behind in the drawer that day we left and thought we could leave for good—so they say, as we grow old and find ourselves closer to childhood than ever before, even as distance itself in physical sense is etching farther and farther away from that starting line on a September, the opening to our September airrush and not the aftermath of the afterimage, the one we've experienced in successive images, convoluting into concentric circles…

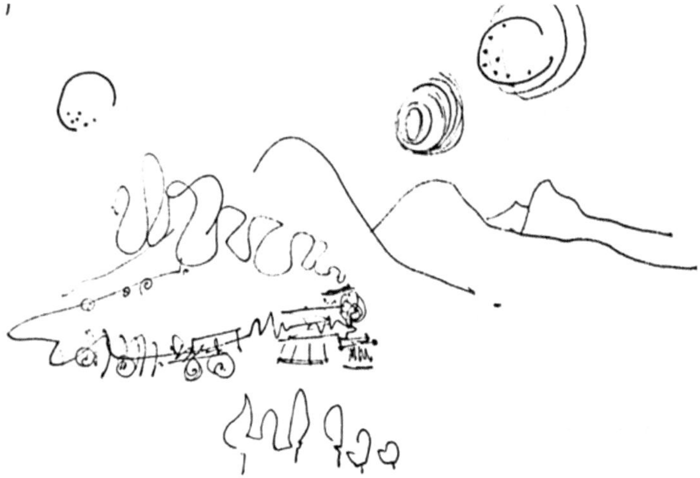

Before the cranes come

Our tired restless bodies
quivering
the way a thousand
cranes ache
before voyage,
before they set their wings
and lift off
to a distant land
filled with only memories of snow.
For now
the passage lies unbroken,
each new of its
own accord—
this is why we ache—

for the embrace between sky and cloud and
mountain and water and

sometimes fire and Neruda's impalpable ash and of
course the
restless freedom,

only to find that it is an act before
surrender

—like a soiled dove we return

bodily unwounded yet
still, suddenly we remember
something that's supposed
to be here but isn't—
it is the olive branch,
or la rama en mi ventana
that we had carried
off before we realized that
love, too, is a war—
and so, we trudge
forward to endless
evenings in the trenches
and carry on with
the allure of infinite tragedy

and infinite sweetness.

Sidewalks immovable

i. I love climbing up to the aroma of clear mornings and arabesque skies, the slightly salty taste of turquoise anticipation as you look down the avenue to the procession of inverse clouds, their shadows walking on two legs on the stretchy pavement where their bodies would otherwise have been and so I'm confused as to how I'd shake their hands since it is their bodies not their souls that are close to where I'm standing—a speck, solid and immovable, on the tetrahedral conjunction in the quadrangle where the sidewalks burn white, so that faces and stories can be drawn anew or similarly washed like linens and kept in a universe churning in perpetual oscillation around the intersection in which I stand in-awe and immovable, on the sidewalks that burn white, enjoying the white of the possibilities still open

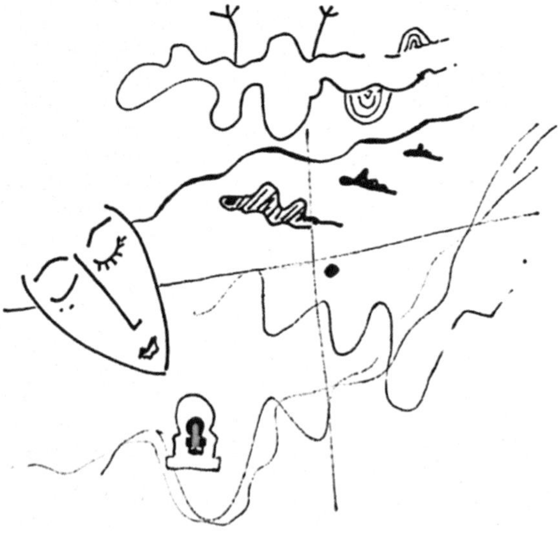

ii. I stand immovable at the intersection where the sidewalks oscillate in transparents, as if the sea is churning its moods as if in an aquarium and the strange waves are kept chained in the glass boxes surrounding—you stick out a finger, and you feel the sidewalks are cold like flesh is. I stand immovable at the intersection where the sidewalks once burned white awaiting the doom of the afternoon when the children come with their multi-colored chalk who seem more innocent than they are, in-disguise of their youthful appearances; and perhaps they didn't mean any harm but the mind shall do what it set out to do and the faces and stories of the passersby start crossing the paths around where I am standing, and soon they will cross each other and collide in chaos or in fate and soon they shall cross mine and collide into the sphere in which I stood in anticipation, they will erase the sidewalks of white and change them into sidewalks of color; and no one guessed that colors equaled pain, as they sometimes take my arms in theirs, as they stamp out my face as they accidentally break into my heart as they step onto my image and leave a part of themselves as they step right through me as if they couldn't see anything

iii. and so in the deserted quiet of the intersection i stand immovable, scared to look out into the oblivion of garbage left abandoned like memories i am too exhausted to sort through eyes open mind blank i see that it is a wasteland of chalk scribbled along the sidewalks that long ago burned in white and itched in silver, eyes open i glance up toward the ethereal ceiling that doesn't even reflect the goings on down below because it is clean and unscathed even in the evening light and it is calm and content as if it supped in optimism and drank ambrosia from a cup of constancy; somewhere along the line I'd like yes I'd like to think it saw the destruction that came on, yet perhaps it was all just in the crossroads of my internal image as i prepare to sleep in the cold of the sidewalks where the faces and scribbles upon my skin-sans-soul give an unsaid promise to accompany me, loneliness as the deciding factor of all, eyes closed, yet in an everlasting hope as an ordainment to keep living, everything burns, suddenly and as if for the first time, white, and the clouds again begin to dress in their inverse cloaks of silver…

The party is over
and the smoke clears
and we are left with only a carcass of ourselves. Not even ourselves, because last eve we had given it all, inexhaustible it seemed, to the fire and flames, had built a pyre to the gods but had run a deficit of our own mutable beings sang a song whose chant we feigned ignorance to; perhaps they'll someday say that it was a dance with the devil but all I know is that, just like Singer said, it had seemed all right then.

And now only the waves of the radiator heat, the charred simmers in the forest clearing, chanting cold in the face of an upstairs window.

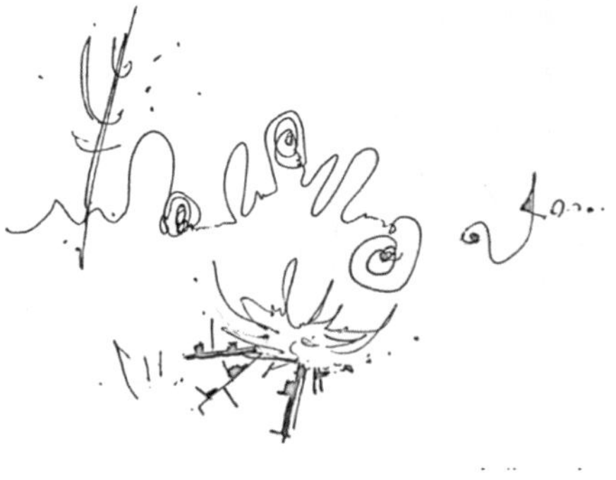

A sense that real vision is silent.
Incommunicable. Indescribable. Exists before and beyond the existence of words.

aundromat Clouds

Shards and silks gray the pines and the cold wind tousled the sky, like the way Cynthia had tousled her wheat-gold hair on a summer's day, yes it was golden but it was still cold, clouds like sheets in the Laundromat tousled loose change and Nadine's number ink-scratched into the inside pocket of them favorite faded soft jeans dancing in cotton, and those clouds they don't even have a clue, they are in that washing machine, twirling swirling by some other mysterious force, like some figure skater as her body in fluid circles metamorphosizes even as she keeps her eyes focused on one single arbitrary focus in space, yes that's how them clouds swirled. And the question arises: what is God putting those clouds in the Laundromat for? I washed the sweater for the cologne I no longer wanted to smell; he washed the jeans for the accidental imprinting of ink that was anything but accidental on his inside pocket; she washed that shirt for the stains, Saturday's beer leading into Sunday, and more or less for the stains on su corazón, steps trampled upon the circulatory pavement steps that she doesn't even remember or pretends not to; but shoes, shoes one cannot wash out because—I'm not sure. Shoes stay shoes because the stains are created external—and we are not allowed to wash out the trampling we make on others' hearts; the stamp is done but the ink stays on the crude rubber where Sylvia had carved a flower in the gum. Shoes stay. Stains stay. And like Cain we must tread with the hurt we have inflicted on others. Our steps go away shadows on the concrete…The cycle is done. And so is a quarter. And in the process, some silver speck of us is gone too. It always rains the day after—think back, and you'll realize it's true…Clouds sin too, someone said. And so they were being washed for their sins.

But all they wanted to do was sing.

Our steps grow shadows on the concrete

Our steps go away shadows on the concrete, small and soft and sweet. The specks of sun like fireflies suspended, once again images in space; some photograph unaware of the surprises christened in air, seeking something, finding little…can I hear anything apart from the sweetness of the silence? Silence like periwinkle and indigo blossoms growing out of an empty sheet of cream-colored paper; silence like blurry vision as eyes open to the fuzzed-out colors of Christmas lights downstairs by the staircase in the living room, as they keep still fatigued by their vigilance stay still by the cream contentment of their anticipation; silence like the sky brightdrifting from the small window to the possibility of a late afternoon day inside in '29, as the steps grow shadows, where the large wooden planks sleep.

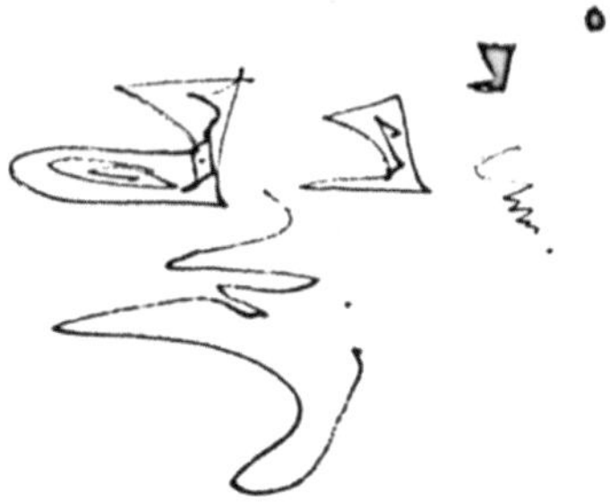

To stand in the future, of our inescapable dusk.

The impenetrable, the intangible, the invented, the remembered and the confused, our desolate air against my skin, taut and then uncertain…unthinkable like the iron city of that picture book whose title I have since forgotten yet whose essence I have always understood.

Again

Again, the exuberance of leaves. again, the sound of cicadas after storm. and again, the infinite softness of the skin, the infinite and simultaneous power and vulnerability of one body lying adjacent to another…yes the answers from the leaves are cryptic and they turn colors like cartwheels in the sun flashing to violettes in December and junebug-lightning picnics in May as the sun beat down on us like dandelions, and somewhere far away the ambiance of a thousand voices chasing down that fleeting oh so fleeting boulevard of dreams.

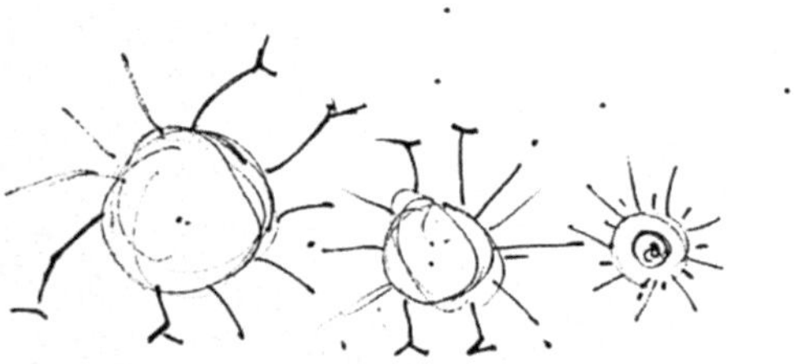

s it over?

Something told us it was over; the fruit was rotten yet uneaten. Someone had come in and cut off the petals and now only stays a stem; a slipper lies alone on a street softened by la pluie, and on the sand there lie little carcasses of oiseaux. In the club on the second floor, there lies an image of a savage adjacent to something sacred, like heaven's sign painted glowing red in the dusk, the glowing burning red of secret lanterns hidden along a side street and falling in the wind—an image of a sacrilege unsaid. And I'm confused, since it seems as if you loved me once, que tu m'aimais. Unspoken and similarly unsaid in languages unsung, I don't care as long as I can continue à croire or stay à space-imagining. Siempre siempre, fact combines dangerously with imagination, like a chemical reaction awaiting combustion. Scared overriding confused. Someday it shall all come out and the sand shall fall back into its glass container: only a desk, some paper, and a chewed-up utensil of some sort. Only a stock character standing close, overlooking one shoulder.

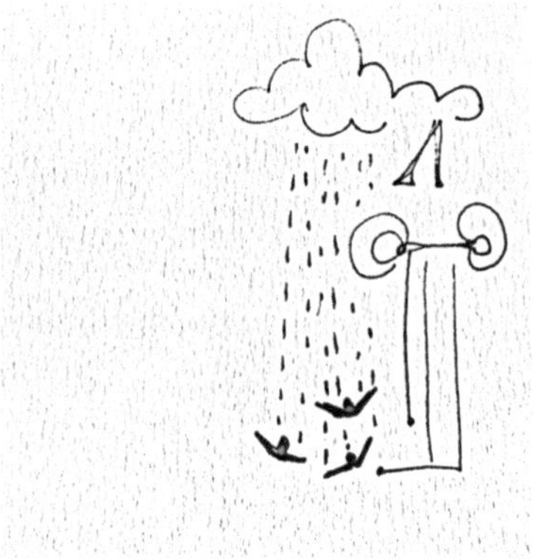

Impressionism

To learn that nothing is quite what it seems through the basic medium alone. It is only after it is *truly* experienced, that we can extract any truth from it;

In the park, the swings are still swinging, haunted by the warmth of a body earlier filling up the space in a gray-misting afternoon dilating our world and injecting itself into our earlier undisturbed minds and spaces
In the lake, it is where we are standing alone in the dusk overlooking all the voices
Where cathedrals exist under light, each one the same, yet only one under the auspices of blue-dawn-light standing tall, proud, and quiet in face of the true Pisgah sight
Only among the sheets he left empty do we smell him
Hearing the sea for the first time in the shells we had brought home from the shore and our bones left in decay we finally feel the soil; a luxury our skin evaded
Only in the sunset of the disillusionment can we sense the strange beauty of our dancing illusions—

It is the same idea of impressionism:
Once you turn off the lights, and shut your eyes, once you plant your two feet connected to the electric ground, your arms extending violently like sycamores toward sky; in the muted, blind silence you'll sense the lingering vibration that is the afterimage of everything, condensed in a place without light; and you'll see that

it is the impression, not the sound or the image, that is important; and that that impression is not the initial impression but the delayed interpretation of that impression

is it the moment itself that is empty, or is it simply too full of impressions for us to experience in that single moment?

It is fitting that the setting is twilight—a time of day with its own strange silences,
one of unspoken secrets lying among the grasses, not yet ignited by fireflies.

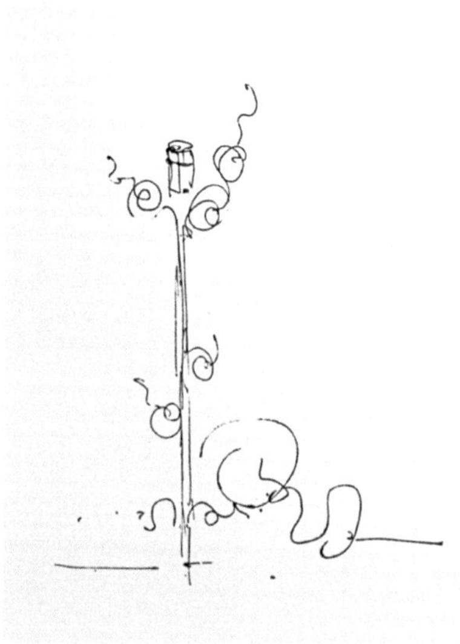

Counting birds

Close your eyes. now open 'em. count the birds as they fly across the sky, bird by bird. sort of like the feeling of a glow of yellow 2pm light streaming in through a warehouse window, shyly but persistently softening the harsh gray ce-ment floor, quiet and without sound, or like that day we flipped and skipped stones smooth like liquor and pale and glowing (and maybe almost pulsing) like skin, in the river fleeting with gold that we could pass through with our fingers, yet somewhere I'd given up sitting in the smell of strawberry shortcake afternoons in the kitchen and Momma's palm Sundays after the smell of cheap beer and toasted lonely blues in a bar in Oklahoma City searching for the light, that'd been there all along. I didn't know. There was once a time when we called it love, once a time when we used tin cans and pots and pans as drums, straight off of characters in a book somewhere. A thousand dins away, still clueless. Should we let go of sounds we knew and loved? Close your eyes. Birds again. This time, imprinted.

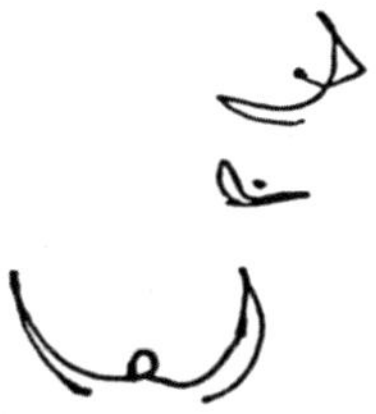

SOUNDS

Et alors il chuchota...

He whispered out to the summer night, open and fiberless without a net to catch it, poetry of the sleeping form…

"et alors il chuchota,
il chuchota."

I'm not talking about an echo.

It's the silence after the sound that you truly listen. Listen, listen and comprehend. Understand. Round and around and around it goes. Smoke like shadows like clothes. Sonorous clouds soakingsoftly the landscape canvas the silence fitting it like a shoe such color of sunsetted footsteps in an empty castlegold. Smoke of cigar clouds that are the dispersions of quickly seareceding thoughts left lingering—above a can of opened cerveza and a reflection not of her face but of the sound. Cloud coming. Old songs caught in the laundromat of old and dormant storms. Yes, listening through the storm. Comprehending still.

The present breathes for a waiting

something in my past made it so that the present breathes for a waiting—
in railway stations and the bottoms of leftover lunch tin-boxes
they smell like fish, but smell like home
in grayed pink and silver*unknown* verses

dance on, little dance searching
not for an "is" but for a "was"
dance on, little ghost turning—

infinite flower,
my shadow in the sun

...

Something in my past made it so the present breathes for a waiting,

like a train whooshes past a platform in September—
never for the thing itself but for something that leaves arms open
and leaves our hearts open and gasping in vain:

sitting at the railway station, we feel the train as it rumbles by, like the giant metal crash of a bird in flight as the wind sweeps our hair but not our faces, a clatter but never a surprise, and it is gone, less than lightning, but only the slimmer visage of a momentary fear or is it a momentary pleasure what did we expect now clapped to quiet, and slowly, the hair returns to the wait of an empty waiting

And we are but Modigliani, stone faces in a surrealist painting, static and cold, in anticipation bound by the tragedies of forgone expectations, so we taught ourselves to not hold faith in order to not be deceived.

the coming and going, and the certainty of that coming and going, and the transience of the trains beneath the paper moon; for that was all, and perhaps the - - awaiting - - (waiting) was the only certainty that life did offer

like a tea kettle that has blown its story, like a train whistles before it departs for another land, like the colors of an orchard
now filled with snow

and we are left tasting the dilution
upon a deeper syrup of stories untold.

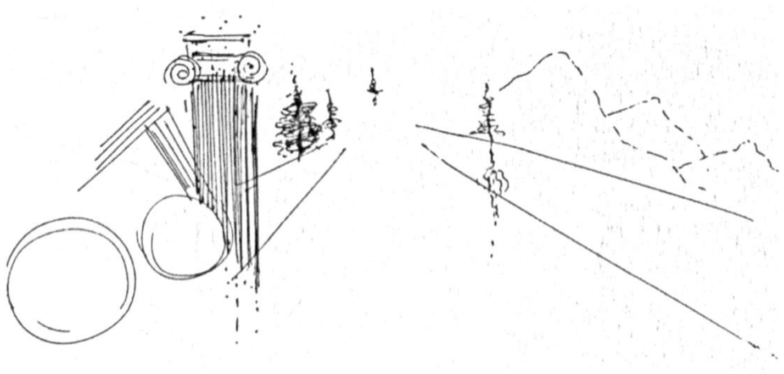

La salle des pas perdus

It was the emptiest sound I'd ever heard. Linoleum floors. In an empty space. Even the metal shells of giant still-born caterpillars inside the gates that closed for me ne bougent plus. And my shoes had been the only ones sinking, echoing like an omen across floors.

Yet the omen had already been pronounced and gone. And the giant gates had long been closed to me, and me only.

Even more desolate than being stranded in surprise on a desert where there is at least sun and imagination of water. Here, I had been so close to life—to the journey and the destination. Shunned, it turned me away without a word, without even so much as an acknowledgement. *Did I miss the omen when it came to us?* It had left early, sans goodbye or the tenderness in lover's eyes as they leave for a distant place.

Unlike even the places, the castle and the fountain, the plaça with the lanterns, the cathedral that came from a cauchemar, each contained in itself something of me as I left them for another.

Ils m'a disaient que there was no lock, that I could not open it and it could not open for me. Until tomorrow, they said. Too late. Already, the birds had started swirling. They came for me—their hollow echoes arising from somewhere high in somewhere low; they came, invisible to the air, something created by the devil but not from his origins—which had once been innocent.

And I could not pretend to be what I am not, cannot see what others say they see. I can only see what I saw. Can only say that I believed when I did, but not when I became disillusioned and far away from you.

I closed my eyes to drawn silence, and prayed as I fell down, down to the linoleum floors. Did the sounds placate? Did they leave me standing?

In la Franca, close to the hour of departure, the platform had become solid and not a stroke of finesse like a journey in search of a destination. For that, is pleasure. To stand outside the gates, to be locked outside in stillness, is only an empty carcass that sings to the sound of *oiseaux*.

It was the farthest away I'd ever been to you.

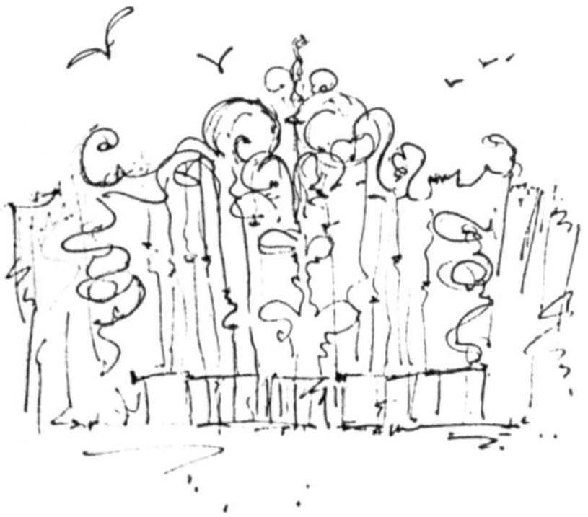

Casualties

Carrying the souls of those
who have lost their
power of speech.

To fly away, or simply to sit—at a third floor window overlooking the street. At a chair, near a furnace, near a window; fixed, inarticulate, immobilized. Eyes staring. Only the snows drifting, sweeping motions downwards, covering all that didn't need to be seen. Snowing inside, covering all that should have been seen.

A blanket, a rug, a quiet quiet furnace with thinking coals.

And it seems so far away—church steeple rings of such jubilee, sounds of caroling bells suspended above streets above snow. Inside chanting silently—*j'oublie, j'oublie, j'oublie.*

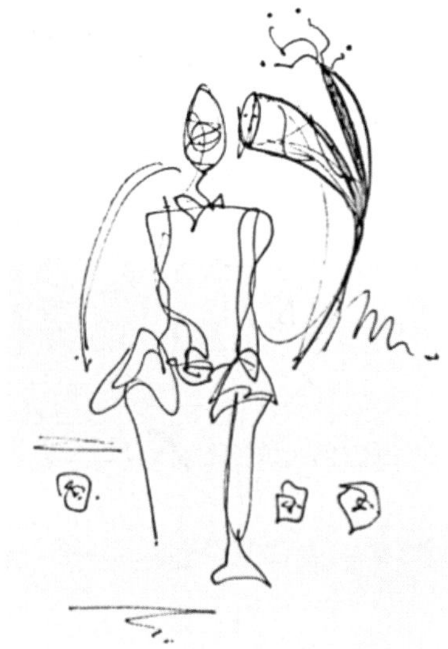

Opposition

and who gave them a right to disturb the silence?

I had left my spot and there, he was gone.
The light incandescent, collapsed, expandable. but where was it breathing to?

To meet at a climax of sounds unseen,

and perhaps unheard,
in a garden half-lost in shadow. So
spoke the benches, lost in opposition
of their own slumber:
a haunted clearing, faced inward upward to sun—
vertical extended, they fell to in conversation
one facing east and another west,
your tension behind my own.

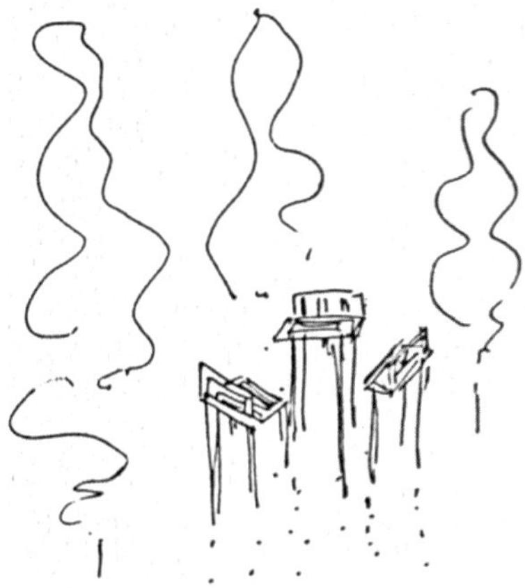

Stitches

It started—a ring in my ears like from an embermetal city the rapid clunking motion of utter and confused destruction facing no-where to go we plunge downwards in a continuous spiral pass the nexium of intergalaxies and we sink forever into the dirt of the ground it seeps into our skins opens up to accept what it couldn't before quenching our thirst and we become one like earthworms in the dust it feeds us and feeds our skins we have some-where to go if only downwards deeper and deeper into the core of our sins that are actually beautiful but once brought to the light we have to become blind we force ourselves to be blind and our eyes close inwards like stitches like under Carmen's tree in the courtyard in the city; such red gaso night in Arizona chill, why won't you let me go? Suddenly a change—

Farther than anything

and to sacrifice the stars
to hear it better.
It was
to listen through the fog, as if somehow desire, could bring it closer. Little did I know, departure had already lifted its feathers and set sail, and the same smile, that you smiled, had rolled down its shades to the other land. This voice had once sang to me of paradise and only showed me of life; yet how could I blame you? You had brought me closer to the Garden than I'll ever be alone.

Will you ever teach me the "cadence" of rain, the "rhythm" of laughter, the "grace of imperfection"—our secrets unlocked by storm?

Farther than

anything

as the morning brought in the tide—the rumble of salvation of which you sang but never believed; and it was no longer some dry empty echo of a promise
that I lingered on
and you pretended
to forget.

There was a time when you made it real but all our dreams fell to like words on paper; and only the time between the beginning and now is where we existed.

There was once an image and I blinked to see it clearer; once a rain and I kept still to feel it better

but all in my mind.

And now just *sotto voce*: soft as a guitar on the emphasis of shadows silence louder than an empty stage and *still*
farther away
than anything.

Ceux qu'il garde...

The things that play upon it, they speak—
But the things it loves, it keeps.

Like the notes of the mistral blowing east from the isolated rooftops of that village embedded, the one we found quite by accident, side juncture high on Olympia Οδos and forever; on the mountaintops stiff and cold like a coyote's scream, playing with the Spanish tiles, like keys, like scattered keys on ivories, so red and desolate and lonely;
It falls, and then
disperses…
disperses like a whisper on the wind,
but doesn't fade and leaves parts of itself suspended, into a valley too crisp for bells—and for that reason it is silent. It is holding on

to something we do not know, something which Sound would but distract. The things that play upon it—the mistral the Spanish tiles the dogs with their shaggy coats—they speak; yet the things it loves it keeps locked into silence, two centuries of solitude caught suspended into its orb, its limbs infused in secret—
ceux qu'il aime, il garde, dans un silence trop immense pour
ses collines, ses cloîtres, ses cloches, et ses folies.

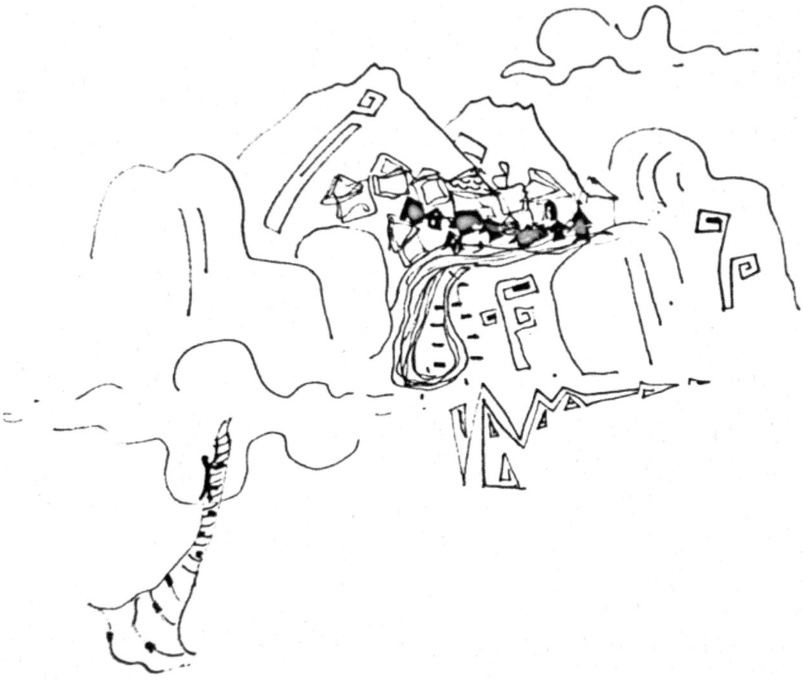

Amphitheatre

I listen to indie music in order to induce blue shadows of the space of summers' eves, the coolness and the calm in loneliness that we seek in all clean-well-lighted-places in plaças of the lanterns and the people left behind and the turned off residue of lit gas lamps as they exhale slowly, like a thread being drawn from a midnight tree…;

I listen to guitar strums in order to invoke the sounds of rain, falling like liquid beads streaming like silk pebbles under the sun running lisamente through my hands; images of the continuity in variation, sonorous and invoking;

I dance to songs that prolong the emptiness, of being alone amidst a crowd.

Music transforms us, day into night and night into day; yet in the end, we do not know how much time has been traversed in footsteps wet with rain. In music, we travel not across time, but across space—to explore the depths of that space, and to render it lonely.

How much distance can we surpass in the infinity of an instantaneous moment?

Somehow it always is that we reach for that depth within ourselves, to a well of things unknown yet somehow always existing. *There is a river flowing strong in the subterranean reaches of our own cosmos, expanding in depth or in breadth a single moment in horizontal vertical streaming*, a reflection in the mirage of the auto-singer overheard.

Breadth, depth, of the substance of bread and death,
and always the acoustics of an amphitheater, suspended within ourselves.

To think of all the footsteps, ones that did not find but were lost, some forever, and to think of naming a concrete space after so many, infinite intangible things that belonged to so many more infinite intangible souls. There are no imprints like there are on sand (even those stay for a second before they too, are washed away), but only the *clacks* of heel and leather, of linoleum floors and in America, yellow piso mojado, little clacks that bounce off the marble columns and walls, but do not resonate; it is a short clap a *palma clara*, but not a clap like that of thunder, for as soon as it appears one spark on the floor before another, it ignites and disappears, dissipates sans condensation or any memory of existence, simply vast space (too much space) and infinite ceilings that let in the light of pigeons and anxious clouds…

It was a space too large for introspection, too large even for extrospection, only large enough for quiet anticipation, which in some ways was a contradiction seeing as it existed in the midst of so many frenzied ignitions of sound. Somehow it was always the *clacks* that unnerved me, that cut the cords of my stability as if I were a house floating on helium balloons like in that animated film Up to which I always cried, especially in light of an intersection of so many comings and goings and lands to which we were going to depart, uncertain if we were able to return days later and with the weight of the clouds passed on overhead that sought the moisture of our exhausted minds heavy with the drowsiness of lovers' goodbyes unsaid.

Ode

It's just like things of all things. I stand afar to see you better. Only when you are leaving (or are halfway gone), do I reach out my hand to bring you back. Of all the years I've been here with you, all the years I've worked you with my

hands

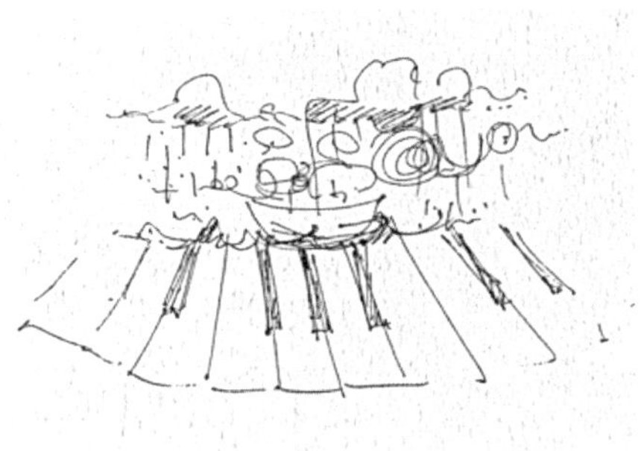

you'd think I'd learn to see your beauty more. But as it is, only when you are quite lost to me, do I see how beautiful you are. Painted by storm, I see in you the blue tempest reflected, and your white keys weathered beneath the hands of mine that speak.

Sometimes I saw in you dreams of far-off places I could not fulfill—trees with leaves like limes against a backdrop of smoke like lavender. Like olive trees our knotted branches grew up entertwined in the frustration of the practice that is; our succulent, intangible fruit still quench the thirst of our eternal audience, faithful long after we've stopped playing; but never faithful while we were, like caked faces on parade.

Someday I'd like to go back to our little orchard cathedral, except this time I'd like to sit in the pews, and simply *listen*—to the sounds of the ivories, coming drifting from your sides, sans reason from my own—only to pull you closer, and intertwine your strings in my hands, once more, without reason, without asking, for we had found that the beauty of the boat was in the rowing, toward the outlines of a horizon we once shared in the distance.

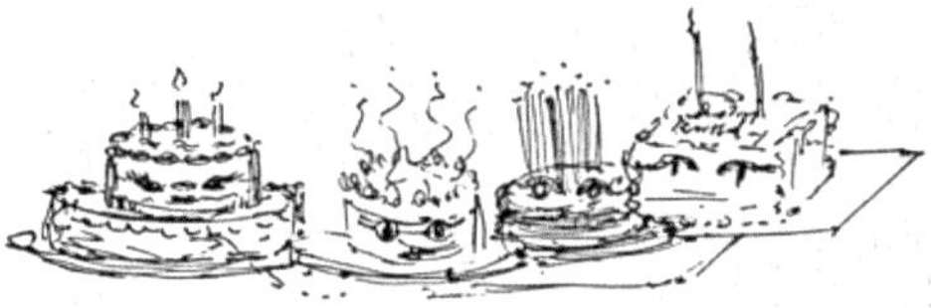

caked faces on parade.

Of Lavandières

Listen softly…like lavandières that sound of laundresses and laundresses that smell of lavandières, soap and water and the fields appearing again across Luberon, the sharpness of the smell, quelle origine innocente, comme cela est astringent et piquant, comme les savons que l'on utilise qui blessent les mains—the smoke and heat of the laundress, the same origin as the smoke that creates the illusions of fields, as our imaginings linger in substance but not solidity, like sheets that flap on a clothesline in le vent…

And I had seen once, in our garden of sails, the children skirting across the sheets, the tall gray-green grasses, the heather and la lavande, as they appeared and disappeared, such sounds of their gray transparent laughter, to catch them among the sails that shielded them and covered them and revealed them as they escaped, in and out and out again, as I stood still among and apart, cautious to join cautious to disappear, forever eager to stop my fixation, as the gray pianist upstairs in his castle cast a spell with castigious eyes, giant clean white sheets attached to sky, billowing like sails above the grasses on which stepped the softness of their skin, shivering silver in their illusion of a valley created by the clothesline and the sheets…

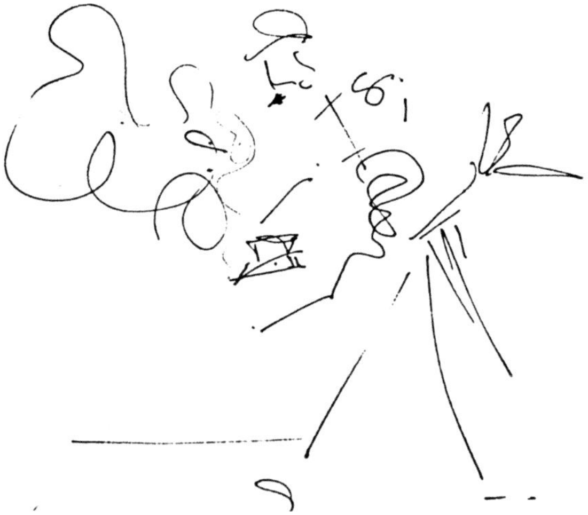

Chanson

Blue afternoons, blue, blue afternoons, how I call out to you. And the quiet sound of eager feet, suspended on the sidewalks leading to Everywhere.

I am disappearing like a deer into the shadows beneath the sun a figure lost like the footsteps of a caravan in desert. So will you come find me, oh lover, strange lover?

We traveled far in order to discover things that were near to us, and perhaps we could say that we left in order to return—

And so the sound never stops, it travels on, even as we stand sedentary standing sitting in alleyways and corridors of coffee-shop bookstores a refuge and a sanctuary but not sacred like the one on piangjiang street with its potted plants among blue lights like stars and unmailed postcards addressed to Everywhere, everywhere but the blue blue afternoons of my tender little blu blu heart.

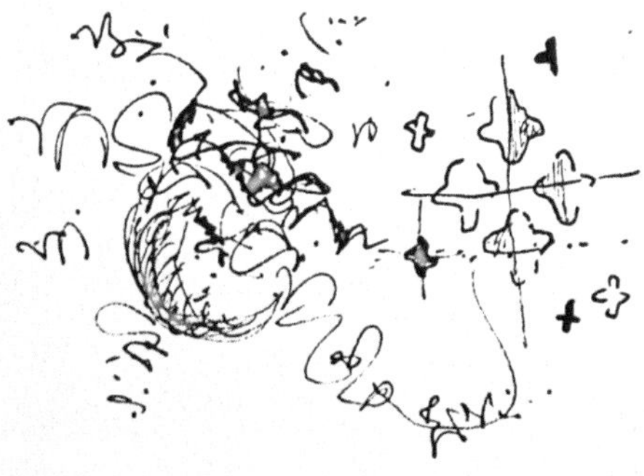

Blue and yellow

The smoke residue of yellow keys
smells, smoke, strong.
Incense of crisp soft yellow pages
caught in its own reverbatory chant.
To its touch my skin turns yellow.
Ah, relief to be found, blue square of blue light.
Let me look out to you,
even as you urge me to look inside.

We burnt and slayed the
shadows as they fell,
one by one like cocoons.

And all the wind,
churning us to static whispers,
gentle and solemn above the pines.

Searching for wildflowers along the side of the road

The gentle sway of purple and white wildflowers scattered proudly and crowdily along the trackside pastures rippled as if by sea as if colored by shadows and changing variations as if by light the pines here it is a jungle in their torn crazed agony stretching their hard dry loose limbs they play with the shadows in their hungry aggravation they seek to absorb and capture the sun natures fuel their raw shapes and primal silhouettes dancing a wild dance in their lines the young overtake the old here there are no powerlines or stones of los puentes or the occasional dead-end house that sticks its face into a square-cut clearing here the dead and the living coexist the white bones of their skinny albino whispers of carcasses being shoved into the grave of the air of the elements so they jut out sideways in the preferable lonely undomesticated freedom watching the speed of the continual train cars whizz by without acknowledgement to lands the trees can only dream of, such speed and such rush for some gold some story unspoken some distant land unexplored, such curious eyes as they themselves stand immovable, even as their shapes feign an eager fluidity, passing by their sad fixed sorrow that lacks even in their unrelenting freedom
the slanted sidelong glances of side street houses with their identical costumes of colorful plastered faces standing like carnival soldiers—

the silver linings of railway platform railings lazily tracing a line
the sad exposed bricks of warehouses akin to their distant cousin roman ruins with their arched windows housing secrets beyond repair
the blue canvas curtains sprinkled with neat sienna stitches, shabby but bundled tidily, as if trying to prove something and succeeding
as the grayblue dusk of the curtains fade slowly into the grayblue dusk outside as musty as curtains are but with a loose sense of wandering forsaken l o n e l i n e s s

…somewhere Cavatina sings sweetly, not a word more needs be said.

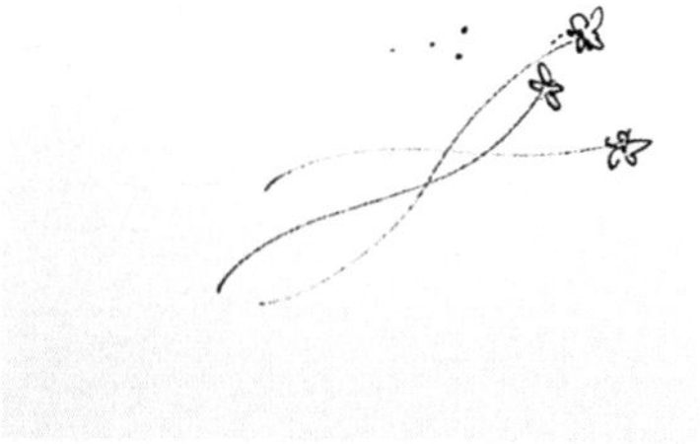

Silence

It is

the silence of dust
of the boudoir
by the scented alcove

an arrière-pensée
caught in the shape
of an arrière-voussure;

its own layer
of gossamer ignited

soon brushed away

the silence of
inexhaustible stars
scattered
across an
immutable
sky

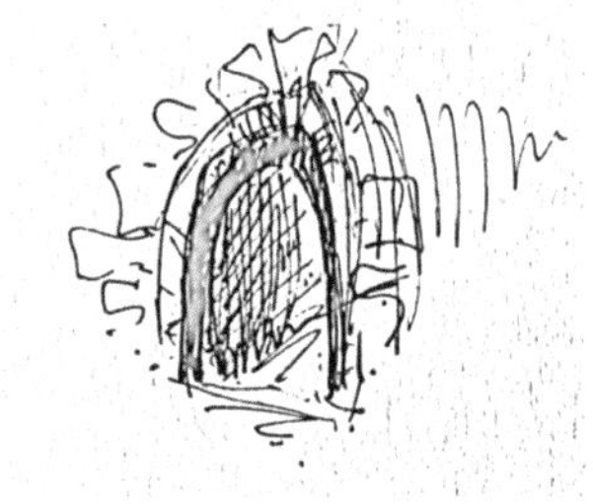

Arrière-pensée (n.)—a thought that is internally expressed, in the shape of an arrière-voussure

Yet the silence that persists uncovers the temporary veil of every fairytale and every "castle", and the stories we imagine to have heard become only images—Calvino's tarot cards confused on a table, or photographs of Terezín lost in black and white…they cannot continue to replace the reality that we had already lost, years and years ago, somewhere prior to crossing the forest.

It is like an echo that stretches on, long after the sound itself is relinquished—it is this echo that lives on, dans nos esprits, nos cœurs et nos âmes, the echo and not the sound itself. Strange, the substance of dreams, how their sinewy threads albeit invisible could be stronger than the substance of actual existence itself. It isn't even the question of true life being "elsewhere", but the question of elsewhere inter-mersing itself into the loom of the actual—solidified, it churned its invisibility into thread, and carried itself on the loom of los Mapuches even when the actual could no longer.

Soft concrete

Inducing the rhythm of jazz in headphones without listening, outside the blue of twilight closing in and opening out, belly down on grandma's covers since she's been gone since last September and in the other room green bean soup wafting like the moon of summer air and outside the sliding door the veranda with the mosquito nets and the actual moon coming over where children scream as they scatter come together and hide away and it echoes inside soft concrete city walls and they fill up the air where the smell of soup leaves it empty still and she is still inside her own mind even as their minds combine as part of hers clear day clear skies and finally about time the curtains draw to a close her dad's favorite sort of blue the kind painted by twilight whistles along railroad tracks or the one hanging above the opera house before start of the show, and even with her headphones in and memory erased she can't help but open up to the

sounds of children playing outside her window, until they too, disperse, and the farther away they go the closer *it* comes to you—they come and seep into your headphones to stay, and you start to hear without listening, start to feel without trying, without remembering or forgetting.

Cadences of sky

And what do we know about giving in to the cadences of sky?

In the afternoon God was making a tea of roses just like the Arabs did in-between slumbers of golden light; the sound of the rain relentless, the thin-syruped consistency pulling the strings of my sorrows tighter than honey hardened onto a stick

Stand clear of the sky for it could let in so much light as if to blind us like white paint pouring out from an interminable bucket
Stand clear of the sky for fear of it falling slowly, all the density of the gravitas of our chagrins suddenly deflating like a giant white tent that covers our eyes, or a sea that does not stop sinking;

Yet we had once believed it to be weightless, boundless, free, just like we once believed in mountains made of smoke; immunity with no memory, such ignorance not making us stronger but rather making us more susceptible

And what do we know of coming back soaked in rain, of having so much courage but so little strength to sustain it, of having loved but not having lived, having sung but not having the chance to just,

listen

to the hollowed sound of voices caught in rain,
the hollowed-out sound of voices caught in the absence of…

Sounds transcendent from rain unshielded.

SMELLS

Cymbals crashing

So far from the sea but someone in some story said once that on a clear eve of stars after a storm, one could still somehow smell from inside—the salt-edged vagues crashing upon the shore, somewhere below and somewhere above, cymbals of la douleur seeking their own constellations.

"Is there a sea between us and the continent? Yes there are rhododendrons in the strand and mammoths in Picadilly, but is there a sea between us and the continent?"—

So she sat there, autumn light blazing cold like a fire caught in ice, as the waves suddenly toppled and crashed and filled her chest cavity of a cave, swelled up stinging like saltwater through the stone cracks of her nostrils, levees of eyes gave up or gave in and fell like una cascada, and carried on. No citrus this time. Only a drowning in reverse from the overflow that arises from somewhere inside. No citrus and only saltwater, and the tingling sensation of a consciousness submerged below the sea.

Sure, there is a sea; one that is, that isn't, one that is, that wasn't before, now 20,000 leagues deep and wide, ever increasing like the continent itself, and what had been is now only what could have been, and simultaneously what may have been, you see.

And her eyes. Her eyes like the sad portholes of an ocean liner, casting side glances dark yet insignificant—simultaneously erasing light and seeking light;

Out across to infinity and to white sails of illusions.

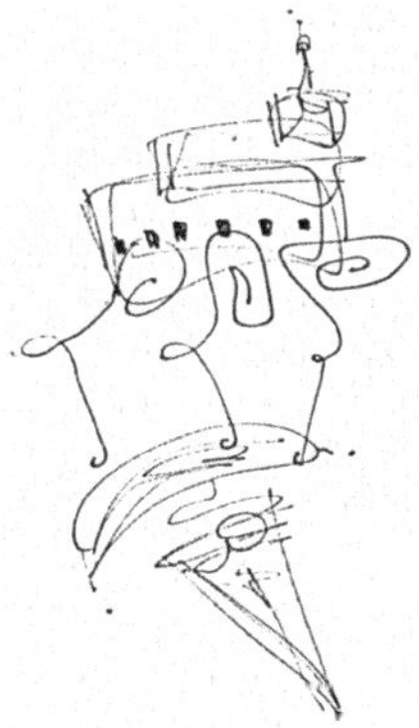

September airrush

Do you remember, what a September airrush we had? Amen, even the rains had come, and left us speechless. Somewhere beyond Virginia's hills and our dried wildebeest prairie of straw and daisies, our gray linen dresses rough and slender left chasing in the storm, and we were two little shadows askew beneath the clouds so somber and lightning so inviting, such thunder as bade one cool hand to rest feverishly upon the brow—

one cool touch now, bids me remember.

Do you still smell, that indigo, dusky cool-driven driver of the air, sifting up of earth and flowers, see the speeches that inadvertently fell into our hands, see as the speeches pass on by just as I saw God's shadow pass on by, one solitary soul carrying up all of ours, or so they said, sunny-Sundays-of-clover-and-golden-alabaster-suns-soaked-across-in-sweet-liberty that promised to know none of that sweet overflowing sorrow that quenched our fields and our souls in its stead. Perhaps sunny Sundays knew it all along, but they just didn't tell us how hard the rains would come down, how fast our gray linen dresses, just waited until we ate the pomegranate seed ourselves. Never had such rain quenched thirst so strong so satisfying such dry thistles a dream as parched as the fields, and in our fever long-awaited, we had drank without hesitating to think of the consequences.

Amen, for the rains had come—

Yet so had the clouds.

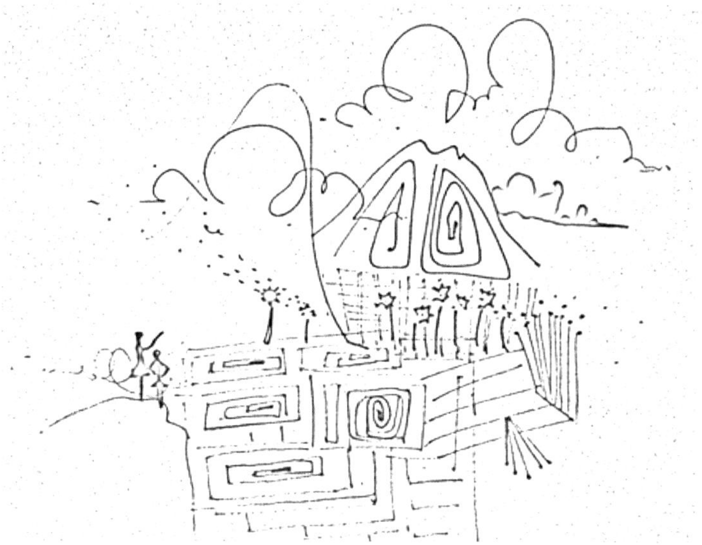

Something more sinister, and less sincere—all the more wholesome and lovely as a cause of it.

She had the strange sensation of spying into someone else's house, sans consent, as she pried open the little wood-like shells; they were thin and thick at the same time, felt like leather and ripped like bark. Smells of musk pervaded their rooms—influx of old photographs seasoned by sentiments of gray and polaroid and attic smells coming close, like the scent of the old green linencloth curtains as the cherry wood laminate floors brought in the rain from outside. They were for her what kidneys and livers were for Leopold, for there was something grotesque about them—shaped like cerveaux, soft and wrinkly, inherent intangible form locked inside ugly tangible form, something strange about the way they came roasted in the little airdried packages with the interestingly colorful and obnoxious characters. Like a little animal, fleshy and strangely organic, living but not necessarily breathing. Is it still raining outside? someone asked. She loved them but they didn't even remind her of Christmas the way she said to everyone that they did.

It was; yet all she could listen to was the sound of a soft a7 chord stuck somewhere in-between chews, swallows, caught between sounds of rain and the seeping graygreen moisture, crunchy yet soft, decadent yet unsweetened. In the right temperament it was sweet, fragrant, like the old perfumes left on the antique boudoir slyly invading the white small-flowered wallpapers of the child's room and gave them ½ life, old and sweet, mature yet still innocent. Earthy, musky, somewhat gritty.

In the small winding streets around dusk in the French quarter, in one side street devoid of restaurants or shops, one that connects one street to another even though itself one could not see, a couple little corners turning at an angle from the base of the creamsoaked walls, showing some iron pipes jutting out like ribs from the basement adjacent, exhaling warm, had-been fumes from an unknown café a spider street away, *comme une cigarette…*

Caught in crepuscule, the motion of going through these little streets—long winding exposure and aftertaste of imagination—synchronized exactly with the chewing of a chestnut. To come from something so small. A chestnut, dried yet damp, it reminded her more than anything of the earth after rain, somewhere lost, underneath the mosses that sink in all the wetness yet does not drink nor drown. And it was the deep damp smell of all that was close that attracted her, the lingering aftertaste of ancient carpet soaked in peach and almond tea and left out in damp clouds to sit and dry, and it seemed as if the little leathery shell with its artificially-cut-slit housed along with its secrets, her secrets also.

Condensed in a density that was akin to that of layered moss, its character intrigued her—despite it being so little. And it smelled and sounded like Dolores, or at least her chestnut-colored skin. So condensed yet so ethereal, for the empty little cage was only a carcass, of what remains after the debt has been paid. Once one stopped chewing softly slowly its flesh it was gone gone gone gone gone…in fact, it was only a shell, only a shell; like an insect once-inhabited. Like a cerveaux, metamorphosed, only where did it go?

And it had once seemed so strong…

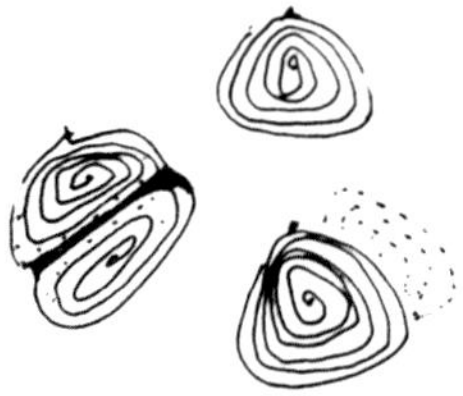

Unsavory

"A heart is perhaps something unsavory…I prefer your body"—

Los corazones son sour and often uncertain. striated by wrinkles of change wrought iron of indecision. Optimistic. still the saliva salts every corrosive organ.

So that is why he prefers bodies. soft and sweet. glazed with the delectable sauces of sin, practicality and solid tangibility. smells of milk over skin in the morning when she's still sleeping. callings of childhood in old skin left lingering.

still warm to the touch, even when el corazón goes cold.

Complexity of a smell

A sweetness. a sadness. one of the conversation of ghosts, shadows, and illuminated light. it penetrates deeply without sharpness; lingers on without existence.

Somewhere closer to cotton, mauve shadows of unopened closets, and softness.

That smell—how could I describe it? It was, a human smell, not a fragrance or an odor, distinctly human but one closer to the complexity of the sweetness of an ideal.

For you, it was the caramel dolor of eyes as it slowly spread-in-smile; a smile and never a laugh; never a laugh but sometimes a silent chuckle. A silent chuckle not because we didn't want to laugh—but because we wanted to, and couldn't. For me, it was always the dark safeness of our cavelike secret coupled with the exogenous experience of uncertainty, as I lay there on top of the covers, clothed in my nudity, staring out at you in the darkness. And I saw you standing there, not as an object but as an experience of an image—only the lamp and the small alarm clock on with its eerie green indication, illuminating your skin. Isn't it true that it was only the darkness, the shadows, and the illusion of the light separating us? A strand in Picadilly. A smell and simultaneously an impression.

And what of the smell of dark chauvinism and danger, your desert flower, or, your gentle vent, as you held me close, as you held me still, that day before you left for good?

You held me by the small of my back, and I was scared to breathe, for fear you'd let me go too soon. And you did; yes, you did.

Questions, always questions.

Outside, dry crackled trees they scream. and I am not sure if I can see the light. illuminating the illusion that I fought so hard to see. Illuminating the reality I fought so hard to lose.

It sifted itself through its complexity, shook itself, and smiled.

Softly speaking, mama's hands, the lines like lines across the sand, her joints like dunes; it is her skin that touches me. Her skin like sea. The white foam that caresses, the weight of her hands on my hair the steady solid waves that don't oscillate but sink with the comfort of a thousand leagues that understand me, for they are blue and they are gray but today they burn with the warmth of hearth and I smile because even when I am utterly lost at sea I can still feel the warmth of the smells emanating from la casa de mi madre and its kitchen with its Spanish ceramic tiles, even while I am seasick and lonely beyond comprehension, like sea her hand to my heart her skin to my skin it simply comprehends without comprehending.

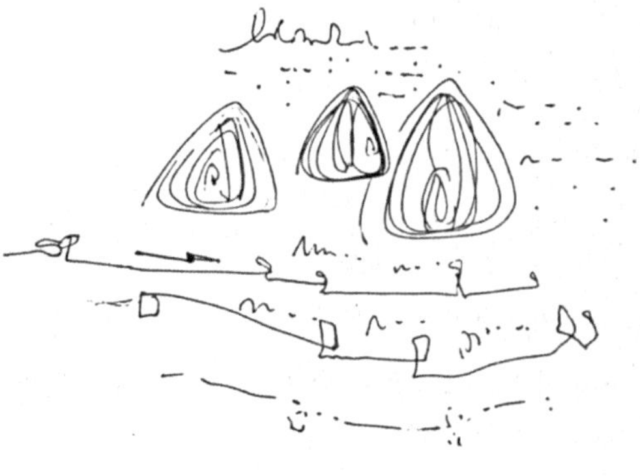

"sand dunes into snow ..."

Longer

—a shadow longer, larger, than light. It is the aftermath of a storm. An echo longer than sound itself for we had never listened so intensely, so closely as we did after the sound itself was gone. In the caves you disappear and recede like a dying tide onto sand but our experiences only solidifying in the fluidity of their colors, saturated by smoke and longing.

Our bones like Spanish songs, smells of the Lancashire moorlands in the summer. Smells of lotus and chestnuts, el pescado y el arroz, well-behaved in their little tin container; playground-mulch days, or the sun drizzling-in softening the eye of the wood panels erasing the edges. Or the time he threw pebbles at my feet, the prolonged imprint of bike on gravel; three chances and two voices sitting outside the turquoise on J Street.

Shoes, eyes, steps, abiding but not residing in time across sidesteps caught in rain. And soon smells of wet wood as transfused by fragrant wood, infused in the shape of a fan, as if it were wrong to open it up to share with others. Images increasing in vivacity, the farther away you are from where I'm sitting. Eyes that see without seeing. Under a white umbrella. Studying sky.

mply

It's funny how some songs simply bring the rain soft rain like cashmere on your shoulders. Of sorrows that smell cottonish like spring, spring sounding of softgraysorrows more filled with longing than they are somber the ones that reflect still my fifteen year-old heart in my twenty year-old body, yellow hallways still clinging to laughter before the pick-up loop conversations simmer away oh Carolina with your hair that would only seem white on me! summer imágenes like the way it comes down to violet and periwinkle strokes (like the Indian tapestry weaves I saw once on a field of geometric poppies and poinsettias in 5th grade, sunset dimming) out across the stadium lights that shine obscure like some spaceship drinking soft beer in a car overlooking the evening as it closed in on us like frangipane and galette on a Sunday afternoon, even as Sire forgot to look at us in passing, even as le petit roi on his golden throne wasn't ours for the keeping,

and in the jungleland the kids are still sleeping and the songs are still sighing the same moon away.

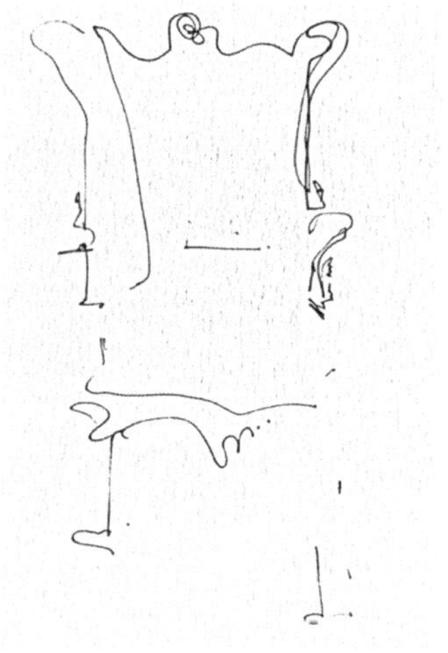

Only September

It was a strange sort of autumn—the sort where the leaves were strangely as scattered as my thoughts. only the smells of orange-kabocha steaming where the strangers lived behind the oaks, anchors of smells that stayed wherever they were staying.

often I found myself going in the opposite direction of a crowd of scampering leaves. giving the uneasy sensation of swimming against the current, quite against your will, despite how light the leaves were or how intangible, like combing through fur the opposite direction, or in the mornings when you accidentally brush your fingers roughly against the side thistles of the toothbrush head, cursing slightly. it'd be okay if I could simply pin down what it was I was searching for—

> As we go down one path, my soul goes down another—*follow it to where it is going for as long as it is going*…le corps it stays inside as l'âme is up above, living its own life sans aim comme drifter, like a stranger washed up upon shore,

And somehow I know—it is only September who has taken away the tourists for good, and left us only with ourselves. September, and it is only intransit-ory, and it is not some fixed internal mistake of my own. that where the scent of September lingers on, there will be another return: back to the start, despite ourselves, and despite the leaves—even if this time, it is only an illusion of smoke and smolder.

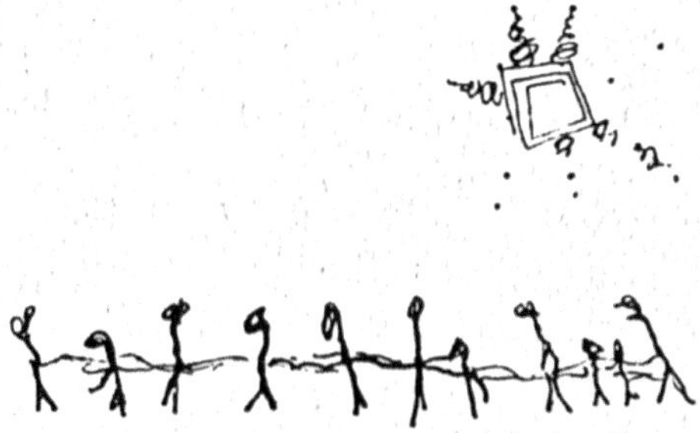

• it is only september that has taken
away all the tourists for good "

Silent fragrances

Essence (n): An essence as a scentless fragrance,
though not without internalized color or sensation.

Extracted from *cestrum nocturnum*, Hasna Hena, our queen of the night, our silent night-blooming Jessamine.

And the image, twilight blooming, of the unattainable…

Strange such forest afternoons, suspended. Such suffusion of light, such suffusion of skin-light on sheets brilliant white in linen. A window, open, satin sashes letting in light, you, open arms, closeness emanating like little pulses across the sheets. Little invisible touches climbing up my skin like invisible daytime fireflies in the realm of disbelief, not forgotten. Their tingling queer shivering sheer quivering sensation lasting longer than an echo, and longer than the action itself. It carries on.
Long after the war is done and the bodies are carried away.
The smells remain.
It carries on, long after the grave is done and the flowers are arranged.
The tears stain.
Sheets, streets, flowers, everything. Always, the echo longer than the sound. Always, the echo lingering into reality itself, but never quite. Liminality. Just like the fence they couldn't cross.
Yet it still carries on.

INTROSPECTION

Chance

Chance—
is a meeting in a side corridor of a mansion full of light.

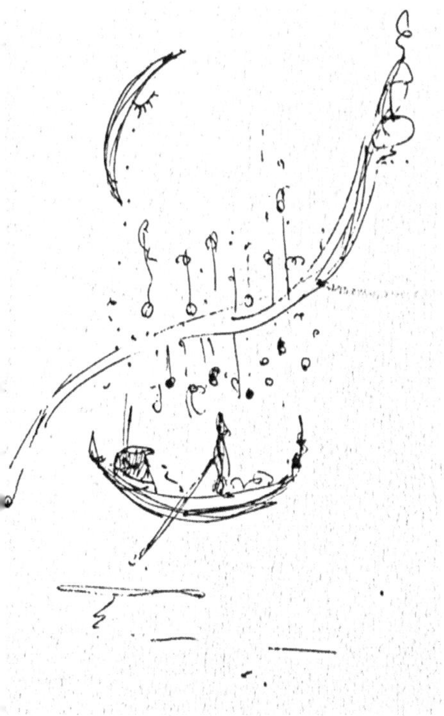

Stations gushing murmurs dreaming sighs of blue smoke silk-screens and newsprint floors, of cigarettes caught and lit by rain, in dry, static anticipation; cold we stood and cold we sat with only our eyes to betray emotion, casting sidelong glances at the passersby as if we stood behind a plastic wall unseen—as if we could see already the fields and the faces, link the destination and the journey, touch the waiting and the anticipation, all the while as smoke slowly encases us in a coffin of our own making...

Below the yellow eye of a single lamp that offers no conversation, so we sit still among the smoke, the whistle and the calling: December to nowhere yet in my mind to everywhere (to Allegheny and Roanoke, to Savannah and Jersey), gray to colors and back again, another painting of my own, dripping away from consciousness…

To appreciate things like ahh "the bridge of sighs" or out on the Sound where a boat zips across water, where all the liquid lanterns inversely squirming, the metamorphosis of reflections; falling slow as the flashlight searching, as the other feet float past on the boardwalk sand, smell infused and carried on like the lapping of water in the softest direction—as you stay still, the winter ahead, like the sedentary quality of questioning souls, so that out across the harbor on the other side, the tiny specks of buildings and human lights, floating lanterns swim alike, constellations of some mirage misplaced…

She stretched and yawned, the yawn that contained a whole lifetime of experiences. And yet, she was only beginning, starting anew.

It quivered, started like a timid yet outward-stretching vibration starting deep in her stomach and spreading through to her arms and her legs as they extended out toward the sun and the stars. It was the opening of a flower at 2am in silent yet eager anticipation of the quiet rolling-in of dawn where it would lie in wait to quench itself in dew it was the quiet implosion and explosion release of gases through a small crater whose origins bubbled deep inside the red soils of the earth the small expectation of the greater unexpected it was the small exhalation a sigh before the inhalation it was the letting go before taking in the smell the profusion the acceptance the ache of the deep of the deep of the deep, satisfaction of inhalation.

It would be her first time. And she so wanted to love. Yet it was so certain so uncertain so unclear still and it wasn't that she was afraid to love but she was afraid of loving. She was so afraid. So often afraid of everything searching.

And searching still.

Sleep again, morning glory

Sleep again, morning glory for the evening you left behind, sleep again among those who shall keep you in a warm embrace; store again, tulip, your orange bulb dresses for the ball where you'd attend to outshine the others; close up, rose, and leave your fragrances bottled up inside, and not left lingering on someone else's skin.

I shall never love you, even when the others shall lose themselves in sleep in your soil. I shall never cry for you, when your innocent dreams are left unfulfilled, or your lover unreciprocated. Never cry, when you cry, your little tear smoking the ashen ground of your little planet so far away.

You have a gift we cannot take away: a beauty of which you are much too constantly aware. One I do not have. You are like a child, innocent and vain at best, and somehow always forgiven.

It is in a smile if and when flowers die, for it is youth and not age that leaves them seeking stars. So often they could live forever, left breathing in the middles of large leather-bound books. How I envy them.

Petals, dear reader, are not synonymous with flowers. Petals are the ones that make me cry. They fall silent out of the sky like silent soft paper snowflakes, to innocently disperse across the mountain at manza onsen, or to sink into the springs, with a hot and heavy, *sigh*. Lonely nomads in search of something lost but perhaps not to be found again: a body, a casa, the arms of another, and another, and another, until you have five perfectly joined arms in starship formation, creating another more free in its collective unity. Une fleur. Una flora. The more beautiful the flower, the sadder the petals in their ephemeral beauty; they are the single most tragic thing, and I am afraid…I am afraid for petals that cannot find each other when they seem to have lost their aim, as I am afraid for us for the same…

So casas of the body are difficult to come by, but even more so, casas of the spirit. They are the ones that continue to dance in my mind, long after the spring has gone away.

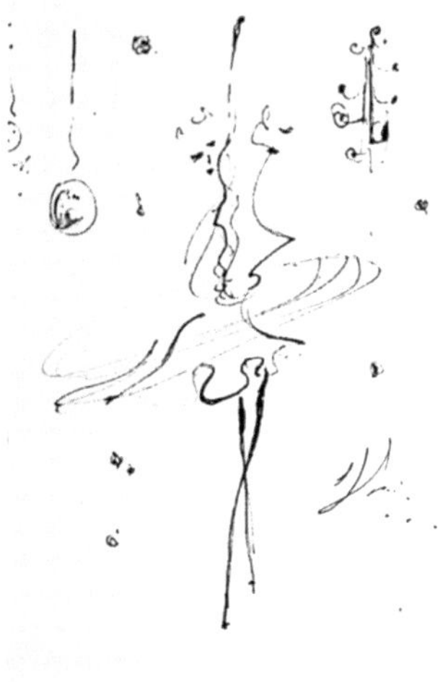

Chameleon

I didn't really know you when the lights came up, and the rosygreengleaned hues start a-singing, their own phantasms under the moving dust. You seem to think that *that* life is more real than your own. Seemingly action-packed-solidified, despite holographic-projectified. The others seemed to believe in you the most then, under those circus suns. (You were so-called famous for your chameleonic impersonations, for your artistry and not for your duplicity.) Perhaps you believed in yourself best then too. *Singdancerain*, holographic green and ephemeral blue. Cry. On cue. Curtains drawing and closing like a smile of another God, cleanercut ordained chapters of lives more straight-edged than the fizzy bleached damaged uncertainty of our own.

You and your many-selves your many-stories I couldn't afford.

I see you smiling, and I know that it is a sort-of-real, and if not a "real" at least a re-al-ity though not deeper than that of the inner. The one that does not quite know what to feel when the cue of a smile is over, the line of the lighting reel is loosened and the tightrope walker comes down from his precarious parapet and shakes with dizzying uncertainty in the newfound freedom of earthbound feet. Only the residue of a greasy blush retained, in the shadowy corner of la loge d'artiste that you shared with all the others: haunted lovers, enemies, swordsmen, comrades—who have lost the elasticity of their story to your own.

Close slowly my eyes. Sink into seat.

I always know you best after the spotlight stars shut off their tiredglazed eyes and all that is left is the dustechoed sound of a janitor sweeping his own sachayed-dance across an empty stage. *Shh shhh shh*. And the curtained smile of your God takes a little sidestage break from creating the realities you've chosen to believe in (is it ever enough for me to believe in you?). It hangs, limp, lifeless, its power unplugged. J'attends j'attends until no longer do I see your physical image. The one you and they know best. Skin peeled away, jusqu'à jusqu'à ce que I can only see an image in my mind, until until in the silence, I can hear inner angels singing.

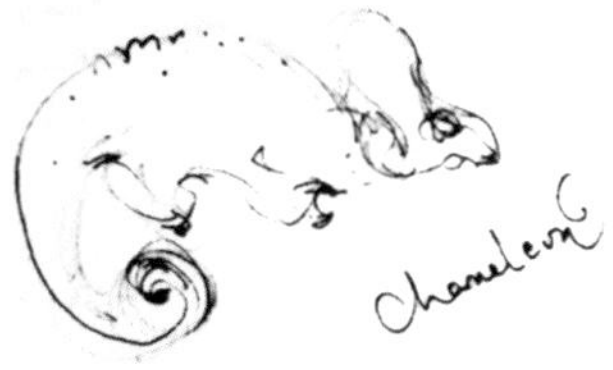

Starfish

I think that perhaps people are like starfish. Starfish stay put and don't usually like change. Going someplace new, we have to anchor ourselves down to something to somebody to feel like we belong and we try so hard to shrink the world down to our size—to make everything proportionate to the size we feel at a certain moment. like the little shoebox panoramas we made in second grade eyes slitsearching to see the little standing figurines silentstoicdancinglight in their shadowy underwater-like confines, where darkness and illumination existed at our will, details of our miniscule world. Introspection—looking inside, exploring; perhaps also to heal. Sometimes I close in upon myself when I'm too desolate too scared too lonely; less space for the fear to creep under my skin like calcium filaments sneaking in and under coral. And the box, my box, is deflated to less space for intruders and more time for introspection, where time and space run synonymous to wind.

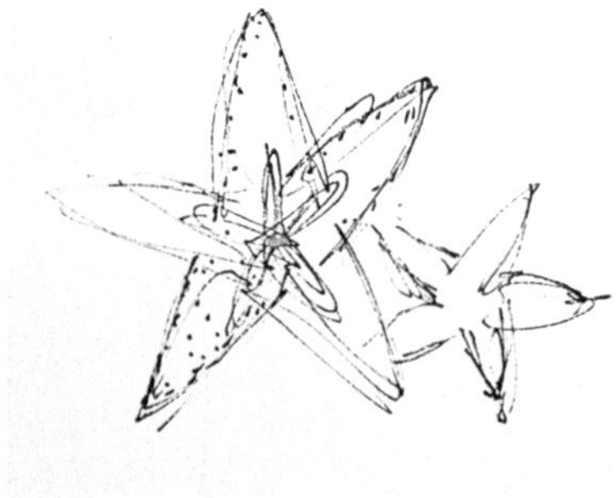

It walks up, to your car, alone—stands outside, like a flower in the rain, and talks to you.

Shelter and oblivion, all one and the same.

It is falling from dogwood tree onto sidewalk adjacent to the window of the one who couldn't see, chose to not see, for you had looked away once I had come up close to you, in the reflection of that two-paneled glass that revealed that we were only one and the same. Why did you look away? Were you shy; was I scared? Only the long drawn-out ghastly headlights of the cars, emerald and golden streams on the asphalt, tails trembling as they pulled the movement of falling white dogwood petals along forward and away into air, as if led away easily by an ideal contrary to their own unconscious desires scared as they were to swallow and to sustain; just the empty hollow of a voice whooping in the courtyard in the morning, a voice alien to our beings and of the stoic calmness of our chagrins;

Again, the hollowed sound of a voice in the rain;
Oh, the hollowed-out sound of voices caught in the absence of the rain

On the stone bridge over the overpass, thinking of the meaning of dancing a dance to the beat of mahogany and wine, to enter by way of the path with mirrors among the slow-drifting lanterns, a slow descent from a high place but it was of your own doing, to pin a butterfly to the corkboard where the tack yet remained of another casualty…

And he had held her, fixed her and couldn't
Let. Her. Go.
Even as the world convoluted swirled sank in submersions conversions of violet and
indigo,
immersions interruptions intersections introspections

Little gondolas of silver appearing
Shifting, standing, shaping.

She dances through fields scattered with starlets
She crosses a bridge of transgrescent souls
And bears as amulet the story of the lady in la lune.

They see each other on a bridge only once a year.

And he had held her in his arms,
She a captive in a cage of the infinite cosmos,

a shelter from oblivion,
a shelter into oblivion
all one and the same.

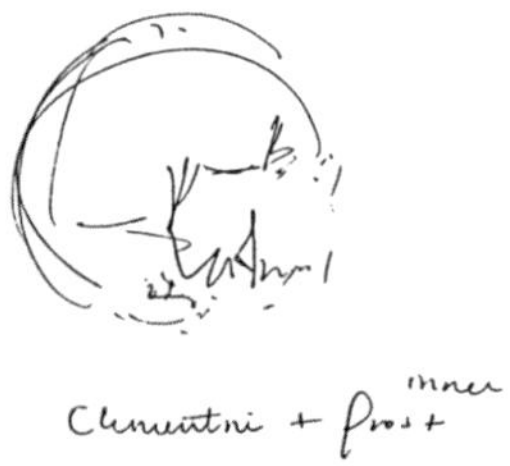

Transgrescent (adj.)—beginning to be, but starting again

Old interior courtyards that open out into light

Old interior courtyards that open out into light—opening and closing out of sync simultaneously and all at once like shutters unable to stop the urge of an uncontrollable wink

Let us pass the myrtle trees and the corridor with two thousand stories, step over the threshold into another chamber, to see another courtyard inside another, climb the stairs to arrive at the red hexagonal door where the two dogs stand, sentinel to sentiment…

And what of the opening and closing of shutters and doors within me? windows into sun and windows into rain, trompe-l'oeil ones that wink out of a secret…the unconventional mirth of a fiction truer than actuality, always satirical and laughing at the inner door closed of sorrow the one that nobody sees. is there anyone to climb the stairs and listen behind the wall where the paint is already cracking where inside an eye is chipping on the surface of a porcelain soul that lies aching? the absence of being loved causing little strength to prop open what was once open, only the strange courage of that same thing attempted which keeps opening new windows new doors out of which I sneak half-opened half-voiced little gasps of oxygen—to sneak a different sunlight into the places I lay smothered in shadows and in smoke…

Each penetrating a little further, each going a little deeper into old interior courtyards that open out into light, like the ones we saw once with their ceilings painted of skies and columns ombré from dusk into dawn all preserved by the absence of the passage of time…and so they are opening and closing, letting in and escaping out like silent Nepalese summit flags—signals that have lost their voices but have not yet lost the right to breathe.

Garden

Someone would've laughed, had they seen me there—Indian-cross-legged, facing like a sunflower yearning neck craning to setting sun somewhere beyond the oasis garden of sassafras poplars and lindens. Slightly inaccessible, it is far above and behind those slabs of stone. Swirls of shadow clouding atmosphere like a veil of a virgin bride, lighting Turner-esque enchantingly pervading, comfortably confusing. And the afternoon's warmth still lingering, like the sea cemented. Hazy hazy my Dolores darling. In the center of a square and its complement of a statue, all shaped by stone.

Little ants crawling. Little to see. To see is to see large.

Sitting Aslan-like in the center square of the stone slab that is itself a square. Empty (but so full). Open air open space but so intimate and so closed. Can you imagine? Être so exposed yet to feel closer than you ever did before in a garden enclosed. And the sense still continuing.

So a garden can exist, outside a garden, overlooking it.

Sometimes I suis curieuse si le garden of Eden existed outside of the one itself. Inside, the fruit and the serpent. Outside, only the sun and the ambiance. And the image of concrete unattainable; the pleasure of controlled longing for what exists inside. A certain peace in knowing that it is there; accepting that it could never be yours. Out of our inherited primal sins, sunken cost of what was already done and over, innocence growing.

Inside. too much temptation. of all that could. of all that could and could be. in contrast. Unattainable, giving innocence to the eye that doesn't desire in envy but simply marvels in love for what could lie inside. sans curiosity of attaining the attainable and likewise the unattainable.

Out of our sins, innocence growing. Outside of a garden, overlooking.

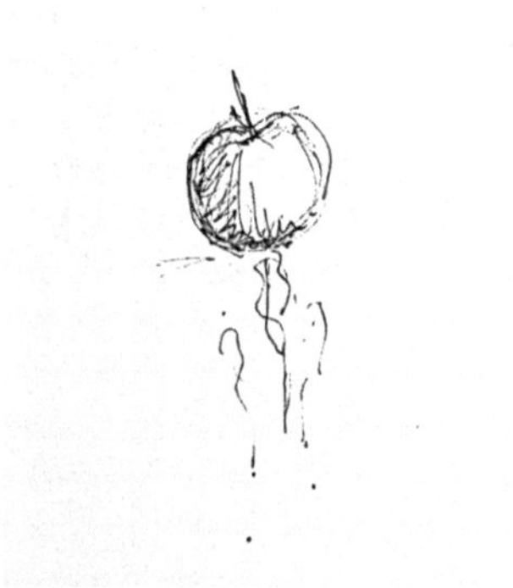

Cars—seeing, looking out, in

Cars—seeing, looking out, in. Quand j'étais jeune et je n'avais aucune idée de comment me comporter. Little has changed. Except often I feel the stares like eyes like stories, searching me on the sidewalk from within.

You, you are unlike the others. *Oui, je sais.* You, you stare yet you search. *Chercher pour découvrir.* You, alone, out of all the searchers, believe there is something to be found.

And I alone of all the observers, said that there was nothing left when you came.

Childhood.

There are places we go to, places we arrive at, and places we lose…only to find once more in our dreams.

And our childhood really just an image, something endearing but quite out of place, like a costume, a smile, or such eyes of childish longing as could only belong in sepia, for to bring it to life in vivid color would make it lose the incredulity it had once truly contained.

In all the valleys and all the caverns it shone iridescent like delicate fixtures of sun on *fruits confits*, the ones that blinked at you sans blinking, in the cold controlled atmosphere behind glass in pâtisseries of checkered linoleum floors where southern Aixois sun desired to possess them in its slow subdued limbs; the yellow heat of afternoons, the white of seaside linens. It tasted sweet, like summer remembered, lost in a photograph or the box of stamps in the cupboard by the kitchen, each containing the internal image of another place. Or the sacred dew of the soymilk strained, served so hot it was cold—for to be iridescent, one must be scintillating: a billion little Seuratian points of contrasting sensations each one reflecting colors unimaginable, each one giving emotions undetectable, as it was up to us to feel the scintillation like a sea in its entirety.

In a way the caverns of my imagination tasted somewhat like autumn too, despite the fact that autumn was the saddest season but this was one before the leaves had all fallen: it contained the colorful remnants of a peace-full summer now made a little more feeble through experience a little faded through the early onset of illness though it was still smiling the same vivacity that danced in Veracruzian lace, now replaced by empti-ness—the complexity of a life, or Ella Fitzgerald on the radio as the splintered gray planks of the front porch whispered stories below your feet.

These objects of scintillating color like the candied fruits on Cours Mirabeau take me far away; in this dilation of mind I am suddenly closer and closer to certain images of childhood which as soon as I see them I am uncertain if they are only images I've invented. Like the plastic kaleidoscope that I won at a school fair displaying a universe of its own iridescent geometric shapes, one I cherished but didn't guard like other things. It was impossible to keep one image preserved forever, and in that same strange sense I couldn't lose it or any one of its images, so I felt free to gaze to look to dream for it offered a freedom I could accept and accept gladly. I secretly loved that it was something outside of my control, for even if it disappeared it was of its own accord and nothing I did could change the beauty of its chameleonic system.

It is locked up in the second drawer of the little pink shimmering chest containing a solar system of glue-on gems—stars, hearts, diamonds, small and large, crystallized and preserved—in their own cages.

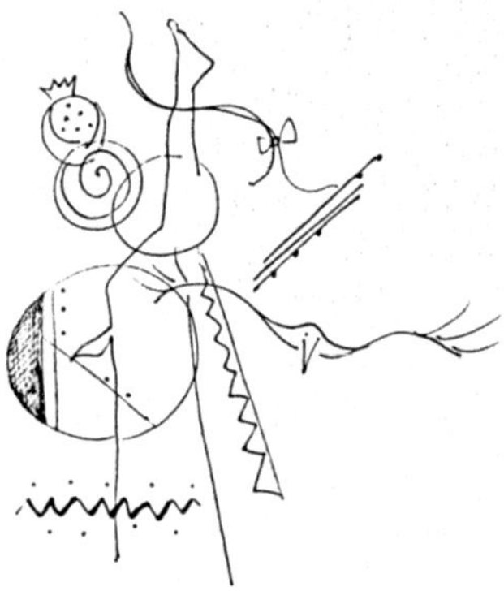

I no longer open the second drawer out of fear out of hope out of longing out of uncertainty, eyes straining to preserve the ideal that somehow it could still contain the scintillating iridescent crystals of the childhood I shed like skin—a delightful preserved pear, dead but still sweet, so sweet, saporous and sticky to touch, still awaiting for it to shine again in the soft incandescent glow of the right sort of sun.

Peace-full (adj.)—a peace that is full, because otherwise, it is only a "quiet", and only one of empty-ness

Empti-ness (n.)—which, in itself, is already an abandoned nest of two blue speckled eggs on the ceiling, internal voices amplified but with no one to take care

Saporous (adj.)—like sap—sweet, delicious and intoxicating like figs in a jar, or dates infused, in the strong condensation of its own richness

Sliding down the side of the
chrysanthemums…
                    it rains.

And it is only the static of a shadow buzzing like a poor electric connection between the corporal and the spiritual, as the wind came, stayed, and left my poor soul out hovering above me. Confused but too scared to ask it to come in, like sheets outside without a clothesline or a dog that has grown too old. Where does it go, this soul, called without consent in a voice indifferent to a physical home in which it doesn't belong internally? Once separated, and never to return, although it has no other place to stay. A stray. It lingers, although the eyes are turned away. So said the clouds outside as the chrysanthemums swayed, their petals shaking in the vibrations of the gray uncertain. Static. It shakes.

Stay, stray. Stay.

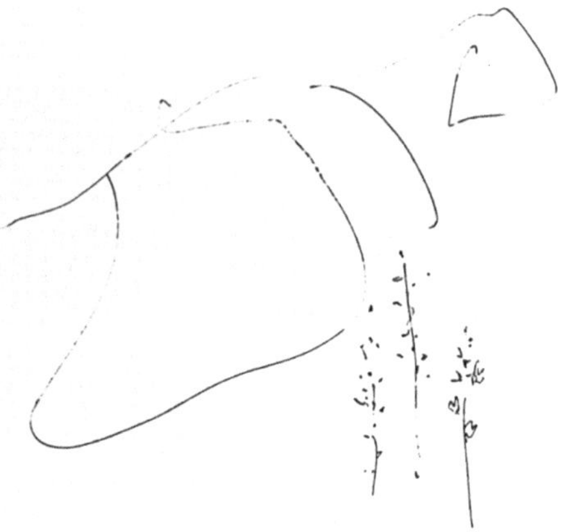

Crying in a safe place

I can only cry
in s a f e place
pay homage to the shrine
of the on e w h o no longer
e-xists
or so they say;
so words spew like names, flames
that rhyme
and your name falls
like grains of sand
catching through my fingers
and I only look and
see that the wind doesn't
blow it away
sifting…

I can only cry
in a safe place
like the camera box
of black turned gold
as they lifted the veil
to my sanity
to expose me
like so
in a crash, a flash
the contraption and that

so-called “preservation
of images”
so it was,
just an image imprinted
now on film
now on lids
now in sleep—
sleep, and silent screams.

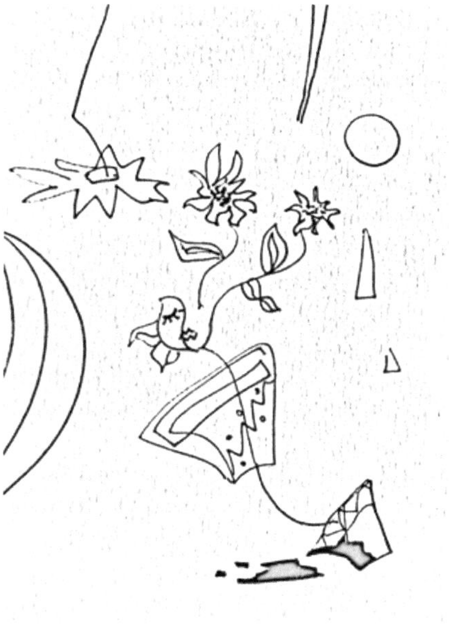

Since some infinities

Since some infinities are larger than others,
some eves must be longer than years,
passing quickly, passing slowly, as the minute hand
sinks
        like a sun under water.

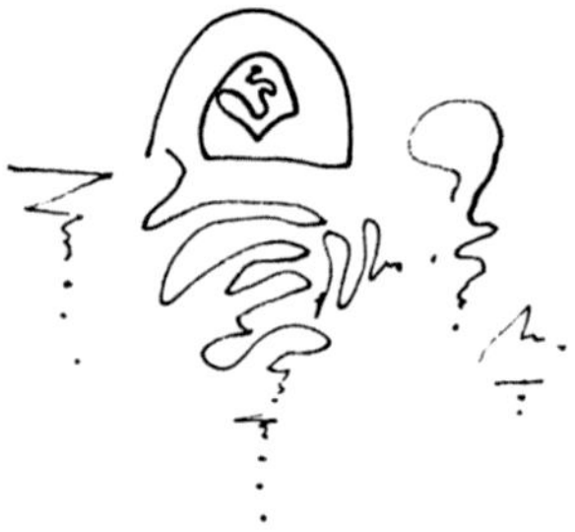

It was the first time I'd left someplace feeling like I was solid. Funny because it was the only place I've ever loved.

I packed the sandwich with leftover brie and tapenade, and looked out the window at the snow.

I had completed everything and nothing, said my few goodbyes to those I could, and those I didn't, I couldn't have said anyway. The things I didn't do—take my grandparents out to lunch on the terrace at Aladdin's, go on the Sam Patch, take pictures of the supermarket with the plastic façade windows above the cheese shop that no one else took time to notice but not because they weren't beautiful or didn't add a lovely ambiance to the unseen of everything, or play tennis on the secluded middle school courts where I used to go to hide behind the weeds that grew slender like grasses…if I could fly down one more time from the field by the sidewalk to the courts and climb up the stadium in stair-step style to catch a sunrise or a sunset, but only if you…how much of the little things become a part of us? Like strips of film life flickers easily, simply, across the raggedy wall, just photos and rain, and never the drama of the Klieg lights against the sky that it was advertised out to be. Somewhere inside we are rebuilding the sand mandalas of our lives, piece by piece, all the faces at the window staring straight ahead, car headlights pointed like fog…Oxymoron of thought and action, and of emotion too. Sometimes, at the climax when we could be most poignantly reflective (it should be called inflective; I always thought that was a strange word) we choose the habit of monotony.

I did scroll through graduation photos and picked out the only one that mattered to me, and I did spend all morning of the moving day bonding with my childhood bathroom and staring out the window at the scene not quite broken by the graffiti-sprayed vans, and I did soon realize after I threw out the invisible cigarette in the toilet seat that it wasn't really my house anymore after that—it was too clean, too cold, too silent to be ours, to be the person I once knew to be true; I didn't even have to look back and say goodbye. Instead of actually sitting down in the loft area that donner sur la sala de estar of the long two-story windows, the piano, and the painting that I called "The Tempest", I just sat on the coffee-stained carpet in my room, and tried to visualize how it'd be like to sit in that spot, close to the ceiling and even closer to sky, safe by the fireplace we didn't use and the side windows with the carcasses of dead flies—just saw everything while imaging to sit there, the three panes that gave outsiders a view inside at night while I painted there in my caveman sweater and faded jeans. In many ways it was just the same or even clearer than sitting there in person, because sometimes when you actually *do* do something it is never quite the same as how you had imagined it—you either twist your imagination to fit along with reality or you leave both in dissonance and leave yourself confused.

. . .

And it was all quite lovely, the snows and the morning and the blues along the snowbanks and the entire snowscape and the golden streaks of sun coming through, and the single shadow of the bird feeder and the lamppost out front and the stones and all the singular silhouettes of the trees…though not of Giacometti...but this time, perhaps, of something softer.

*In*flective (adj.)—(disambiguation) *in*trospective or caught in the retrospection of one's past life

Reflective (adj.)—(disambiguation) to reflect off emotion, not allowing emotion to be felt or prolonged internally

'o metal-skinned houses:

I see the snow today
I see it falling down,
but truly:
as if some hidden hand brushed it down,
and once in a while, lies suspended…

The snow brings me
to the gray pavement streets of Morioka,
past the railroad tracks
and home to our metal-skinned
houses; to think
how we survived like a matchstick story,
is strange.

There's a lot I don't remember,
like the festival of lanterns, or the
water-lily bridge, or the black swans
that reside there, whom I once all
knew by name.
There was that day of crying
in the bathroom stall, a day of roasted
beef and peppers; a day of tissue-box
castles, and other things. In some ways,
I am still
in that big rocking chair
at the park

shaped like half a hamster's wheel—
it was you
who had sat me in it; every time it would
climb and we would fall upside down—that was
and is the closest
I will ever get to sky.

I see it quite clearly, see that way home:
a piggy back here and there,
a stop at the little bakery shop,
a treat and I forget
the cold that screams inside our
coat sleeves…

When I see snow whirling
in the depths of the sky,
I am reminded of Morioka;
I carry the places I've been
wherever I go.

…because our goal is to always feel foreign. To understand with new lungs to see with new heart to dance with new mind unchastised by experience; to use our legs not to walk or to climb, but to jump and to stretch and someday, perhaps to fly…so quiet, calm, solidified, like that first time you had traveled alone only to find yourself in ambient light, not even knowing how we got there or why we came. *Take slow breaths to transition the time*…it is the first day, or the first night, to recall that we can simply use our eyes, not to only look out from, but to also look into…

2am and the smell of everything clean, unity bounded by soft starlight and softer dishwasher serenade:

slow drifter, what do you see?

Cold

Ice cubes skittering on my breath, tongue substituting heat; paint stroking across canvas of atmosphere, left lingering after exhalation: it carves out distinct shapes letters like questions as they filter out onto the street…the complement to warm mocha-jazz, its fine indigo robe obliging. Seeking the sunrise trapped in the cavern exuding, finding contact somewhere below the ribbed ceiling; a sting and then a shower of little metal skittles over and across skin, outside swirls of electric light swirling thin lines inside my knotted stomach tightened in unfulfilled desire; it was a cold cold day, yes, but even more so it was a wet day; the professor in his broken slacks comes in like a cat; all across the quay cars line up with their windows closed and occasionally the smoke from a cigarette reaches up like the pallid arms of a drifter in the stream;

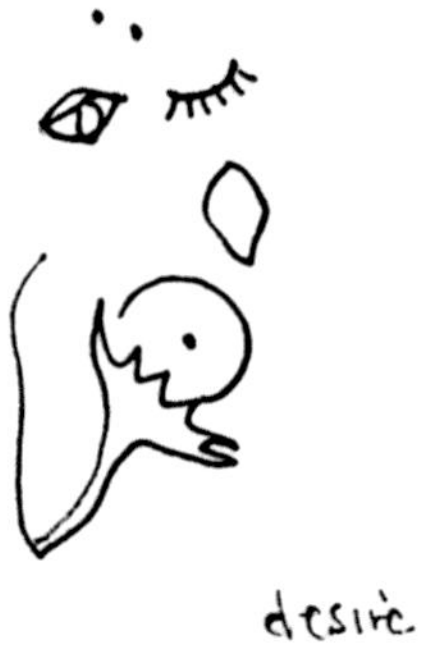

the painter she draws, everywhere circles that drew continuous from the ice cubes inside her tongue, to tie up the landscape and fence it in; everywhere enveloped to an invisible rhythm of suppression under desire, everywhere enveloped, and nowhere free; it feeds on itself, cuts her up from beneath and eats her up inside, but there are no invaders: only a child starving inside myself for it had been too long since.

For if one lets oneself feel cold, invent the coldness that seeps in, unlike what they may think, it is not a passive act but an active one, letting the cold come onto us…Yet as if we could help it, shrinking shriveling into one's own skin.

Something sensual

Something sensual about the way summer languid heat and sounds of electric ceiling fans blurred lines behind where strawberries melted on the sidewalk stand, bare arms and glazes the way it all, rolled, rolled off the tongue and plays, soft patter of tongue on teeth, several syllables in succession, little patters not of the consistency of tin on rain but could it! it could be such soft pats of summer rain even, but it was more so the softness of a languid flower, yellow flower, caught floating on the surface of an overlooked pool, not of holy water, but of a child's imagination caught undisturbed and forgotten; stillness stirs something throbs something pounds deep beneath the surface disturbing the suppressed quiet, perhaps it is the secret growth of a lotus root, or a cancer in the mind; something sensual about the way her hands with their fingers soft yet fingernails sharply colored, lacquer and oil, the way their scarlet softly rolled down the window of the automóvil without so much as a sound, the same way she will touch his chest behind the thin walls where I shall sleep;

and in the kitchen, the way Edelina rolled up the pin as she crunched the oats and sesame seeds underneath…little sesame cookies, for the moment, scattering the stress of such languid desires, unleashing them, and letting them go…

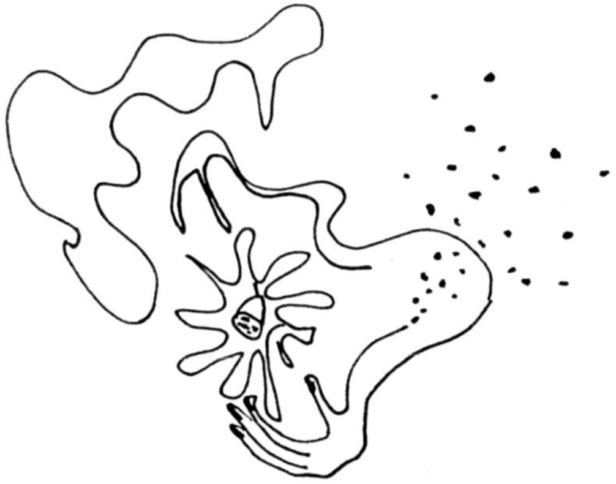

Switching gravities

And it was, undeniably, not stars that fell but flowers, ones that had evidently lost their gravity and fell to earth with a sigh. For what was gravity but a thousand waxen strings pulling one safe to another other, silver poles holding up stars like lanterns, stilts placed in the center of human hands like the lamp-bearers in Morioka, the silver translucent fibers of luffa gourds;

I had a dream once of climbing up an escalier but you had let me go…

A sigh—a thousand sighs, all around, unheard, but one could easily feel their presence by breathing in the evening damp and inhaling the carbon fragrance of their sadness. Swirling air coming from such pale translucent exhalations. Pulsations of their wings shattered after an invisible pelting rain.

They would soon learn of a different gravity. One that centered you and kept you transfixed to the earth, to the ground and the dirt, to the igneous molten heart scared to see light. To the ground from which will one day spring, flowers.

And yes, it was inevitably, flowers that fell. Ones of youth just like the ones from Omelas. Ones once suspended in the gravity of weightlessness. Ones stripped of their virginity. Ones left falling after rain, devoid of strings or gravity. Ones who could not stay standing.

Someone had cut the fibers of the luffa gourd, and the stars fell, shattered, in disgrace. No more transfixions to the cosmos, to an order of stabled constellations. The lanterns caught up on stilts swerved and shook violently, as if in storm.

And still, you stayed standing.

and I was thinking on my walk in the woods, how nice it would be to just -kiss them-
and not have to worry about tomorrow
smoke and urine
and the occasional irises that bloom
by the benches wet with rain
isn't it funny
that flowers are brighter
in the starlight?

well, he got what he wanted and same with you, ha
better to pull the plug now than let it
fuse— di ffus i n g isn't as as it
into sun easy
seems

Overdue

I visited the library the other day—God's library, the one where he lends out emotions like paperbacks, the ones they sell outside church in the summer. I always forget to return on time my favorite one called "Joy" and another called "Optimism". The library charges such a heavy fine for overdue books: two ingots of "sadness" for every second that I am late. These ingots I do not give to the library, but the librarian gives to me, and each time I carry these leaden bricks in my bag, they weigh down on me the entire walk back, each time a little more alone, each time a little more surprised than the last.

You laugh, yet I swear it's true—there is a system, and there are different charges for each one, and somehow I suspect it changes for each person. I am one of the bad ones. I'm not sure why it is. There are ones who, even with bad library scores, simply get to hold on to books and videos longer—even the one called "Love", which for me is always a maximum two week loan. It doesn't even matter because the film still plays over and over in my mind long after it is over—I tend to believe stories easily. You'd think they'd stock more copies of it on the shelves since people are always searching—strangely they don't, and we are condemned on those days and years, to enjoy stories of a lesser fiction.

I never venture out into the section of the books with the gold brocade covers that fall into dust at a singletouch—they are in the aisles with the cold blue fluorescent lamps; there are some who have read them who have never come out.

Perhaps tomorrow I shall try and seek out the one called "Sadness" instead, to see what charge it shall bring if I were to bring it down upon myself—if all is fair, like it is in "Justice", then perhaps for once, "Joy" will be fined upon me. Yet isn't it all a story? But at least to live it once, as if you believed it.

She sat still. And stood up again.

All because public benches are like commas.

All because life is too short to stop living, too long to go by without recollecting.

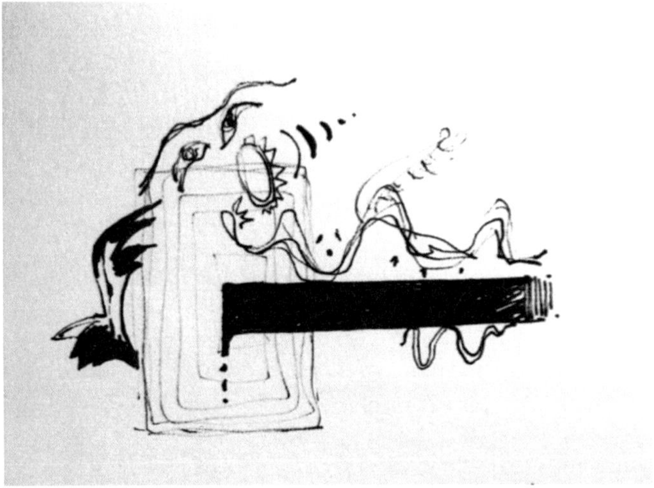

istractions in shape of a cream silk string

Sideways i lay my head down on the patio table sinking dark green into soft of a world close and in slumber of spring. i looked up and saw the silken cream-rose ribbon so surprising to me somehow against the solemnity of a translucent gray sky—it was lying there like a dragon in the sun, extending like a tentative caterpillar of a gesture toward me...a rope, they say, sailor's string, for luring us in…or only to show us. only shall I come? for to come is to leave; to come is to leave one island for the other;

there are no songs that come free—each a siren of its own.

i couldn't forget the air that i saw in eyes asleep, that Indian summer feel, that lulling of two people sitting close, space-stirring, a pause between two breaths, and i, not knowing if he could be writing about me in those gray pages he once promised to show; so much to say—

so much to say and only the silence that speaks, and then of course there are the birds that sing. it was spring. i couldn't help but ask. eyes like Egyptian afternoons as i had thought once...Silence. And the cream-colored silken string olvidado out of the pages; and him writing close; me listening.

Contemplation

I lie awake in a transitory
dusk; awaiting the spring, encased in a whisper
carried far above the groves.

Perhaps it is
she; perhaps it is he;
carried on by the sound of the air
heavy between feathers of birds, suspended in flight
as I sit—
alone—
on a park bench
contemplating the eternal wait
of the blue-gone sea

tracing the silver silhouettes
of their voices.

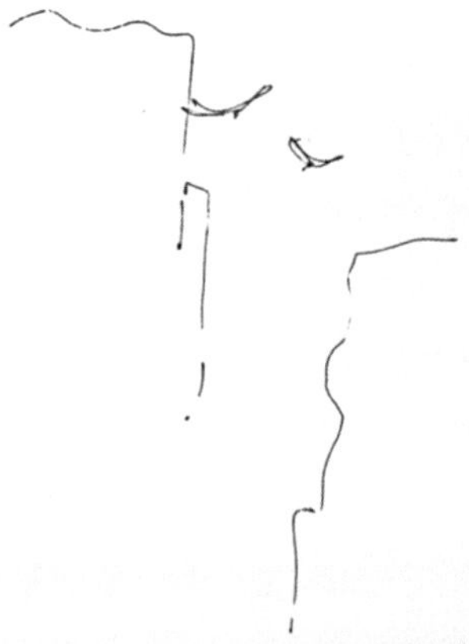

Called Schoen's place in dreams of another town another time. And all that I've inscribed coming back to me; funny how we could remember, all the little things, the way it came across like little pieces of bread softened by the wine of time, little conversations unlike the speeches we'd practiced full of the importance of more significant things. Silly how it sometimes comes out, disjuncted in quips we didn't plan, that after all this time all we could think of to say was the same we'd always said, of so and so and this and that, and the little specks of existence that had never mattered to us until now, when they should have carried little. So there we were, and it was the little breadcrumbs we fed the ducks that held within them the gold of a purer, grander conversation. And there we sat in the almost-silence, saying little, but not because we were mad or had nothing to say, but because we had finally grown up to be fine with the silences…

It was just an imagery*imaginary* on the surface of the Erie Canal, etched in silver and softened by boat foam on the edges, the canal water green like liquefied floating mosses that gave substance to light, streamlines of the sun glossing over water, bubbles that gave mystery and even the ducks who with their feet and winged dance inscribed in fast forward motion the details of a larger scheme that could not be contained, as the trees peered over still, into the depths they could not see, things that children in their laughter contained; and all connected, like little conversations of speeches of things we've said that have been said once before, and that time I laughed when you had answered that it was the last time but we had an eternity together, and I hadn't believed but I'll never forget, that day sitting lost on a park bench by the side of the old gelato place since closed, simply sitting there, as if it could.

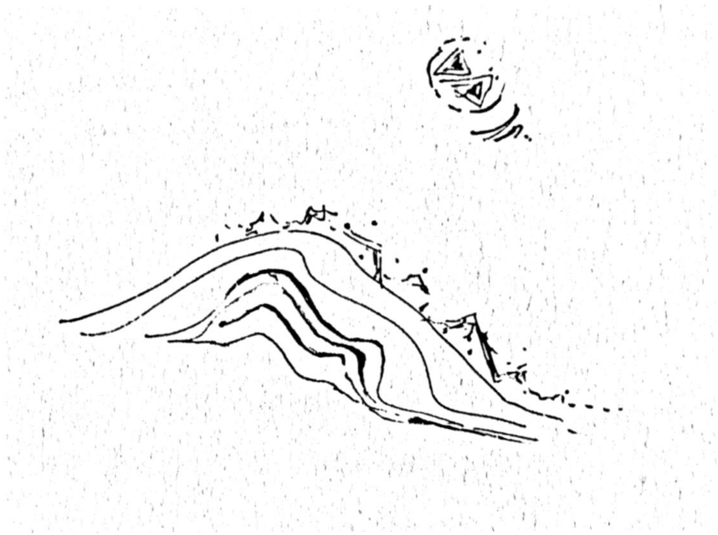

cattered

It is that the intangible was the only thing that was certain. It was all scattered—like autumn in the rain. For once I didn't try to catch it. Like straw skittering across sand, I am escaping from things, but the pieces of myself run into myself: forever, the quandary and the dilemma. I ask whom it is I am escaping from (and at times, it seems like it is only myself), even the emotions drifting like a sea without roots sans depth

or the sunken-ness that keeps an anchor at bay. It was like swimming against the current, a current of weightlessness yet of sedation, and still I held the papers in my hand, sans inscription, the only thing tangible that I held on to in order to prove an existence outside of my own.

The fear of nothing, and the fear of nothing-ness, the latter being the act of opening to a page that is no longer there; there is no continuity, only the pellucid orange of scattered moments; so I feel under the strange September sun both high and low and far away scattered by its own light, that it is something external but also something internal inside of ourselves.

Like a sky with no past of clouds, or a dry sea of leaves intangible. Or a scratched half-hearted note that didn't even say goodbye,
or where he was going.

Infinite

And we cannot say anything since we've lost our voices to the silence but we are neither mute nor dumb; somewhere close there is the stimulus of a flamadoodle on snare a pulse on timpani and the impression of some voice invisible crowded above the ivories like a thin drawn line of smoke suspended above like swings star-swinging—do you remember how all of us used to go out in the gardens at night to capture our imaginary fireflies in a mason jar and count our blessings before sleep, how we used to catch our imaginary dreams in a firefly and hold it up to the light and bless our counts until the day someone stuffed them in a carriage away and we were left to slowly climb down the stars one by one until the rungs themselves disappeared? the swings still swinging but this time it was the shadow of a resolution some dark strand swinging from la lune…that was when we learned to once again appreciate everything from the very beginning the opening line and the momentum of a breath that slurs the audience into silence; the beginning is only the beginning when we start at one, simplement uno because at one is where it all starts, a first kiss or a first glance the first time I caught your eye in the pause of the disresolution of a sentence hanging in an up-curve off Mrs. Drooz's Romanesque nose and round up again to her spectacles searching up for a clue and finding only the start of a question, the first snowflake that spurred everything into creation but what about the fireflies who light in order to relight in order to search back to the twilight that first introduced them to the earth? And just like so, I say "see you sometime", as all the counts disperse into the infinite; infinite snowflakes infinite poppies infinite imaginary Indian summer fireflies…it's comforting that somewhere at the moment when I blow the dandelion's honesty and simplicity into the skinny-fingered grasp of eternity, into her ever-forgiving womb of poppy-eyed colors, it's comforting that somewhere someone is feeling infinite, just like Charlie.

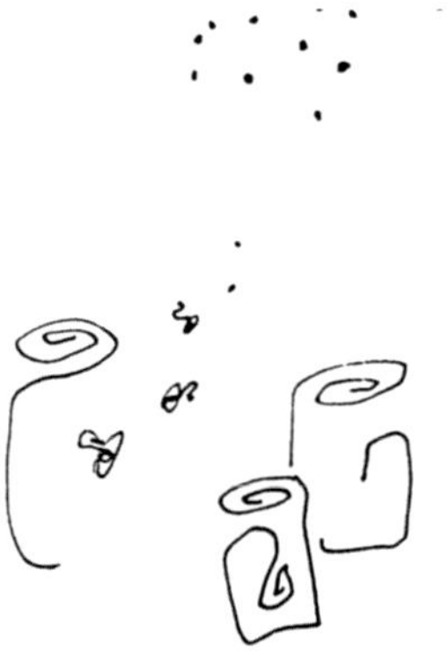

Illuminate

In straight-line-edged motion, sliding past, just like years, lovers could be; misplaced socks and misplaced clocks. Sitting sedentary, I realized how you could feel everything moving around you—that one day I sat in the coffee shop behind the closed glass and outside voices, the petunias in wooden flowerpots and the bench that knew my name; I felt the truck sliding past in the avenue, sliding façades and sliding colors, and felt despite the glass the sudden wind cross not my face but rather my entire body. Sedentary being but sifted shifted, like a desert flower shifts in the sudden desert wind; roots embedded but spirit free. Mental resilience both an effect and a cause, in a physical skeleton inescapable.

It was the feeling of being lonely in a crowded place moving clouds and moving parts, and I am disco blue and swaying slow; illuminated *elsewhere* against the souls of others—*let it illuminate me*—zoom in now on one solitary grass shifting in a sea of grasses those silken prairie vagues enchanting; now seeing without seeing that one could be lost and found simultaneously, because yes, it was the same thing after all—the wind that blows us south is the same one that keeps us still. And still I sat in my closed seat behind the glass and the flowers that have since forgotten my name, chamomile tea enswirling, watching as the years, as the stories pass on by.

Only this time, give me a butterfly net to catch the gold as it scatters.

ome, sleepwalker

Come, sleepwalker, come for you're the only one who will understand me. Come for in our slowly drifting world, the somnambulants are the only ones who could ever be awake.

Meet me in-between the empty rush of invisible moonbound traffic, 2am sweeps and hollow lights, drive out across the plain to distances of where I am standing;

Search me out before the Mingsha sand starts singing before I fly down the dunes one long leg sweeping out before another as fast as a shadow in slow motion as we set out chasing the sun;

follow the sounds of the footsteps after rain,

Come follow as we peel backwards to sun and eternal dust-dusk-dust, the past (and not the future) as the only beginning I'll ever get to keep and the only start we've ever imagined,

Come walk with me along the shorelines of illusion.

For we are one and the same, the somnambulants and the spontaneous caught in the ever lonely sea—

so come, dear sleepwalker, come walk alongside me.

The curtain closes

The curtain closes.
Stillness.

There is not much else to say
Except that which cannot be said
in these letters.

Creativity? You ask where it is.
It flew away.
And the only thing left is the truth.

To get the best, we can only go
for the unexpected.

What is destiny,
If chance offers us the best escape?

But they say, that there is no escape.
Even at the end, even at the end of all things.

And always, always,
the calm, the angst, the forever, the transient;
the music and the beating and the song of Time.

Lights go out one by one on the street we never want to forget; they are lanterns, visions we used to chase but had never straight-held in the center of our palms.

After the flood the lampposts still stood; even as the names inscribed on the planks started erasing themselves away. And someone had come daily to light the lamps, even brighter than before it came. And left.

Something was changing, and had been, ever since the sun started to shine liquid and old across the sea. The farthest lights start to be extinguished, el corazón gasps out a tiny little breath it has sought to contain for so long, releases and lets go in an exhale of a sigh…

as if the lanterns were being puffed out, one by one—I saw birthday candle streetlights, our little trembling expressions of desire extinguished calmly, exactly, easily, avec une sourire inscribed on a face un-bled by the creases of chagrin qui ne connaît pas le douleur…

There is Time as the antithesis of the lamp-lighter who comes at dawn, and there is Time as the street sweeper who comes when the lamps have gone away. I have known both. I first heard of the latter in an old-age apothecary in Stratford-upon-Avon when I was twelve, seeking an antidote to sleepless dreams of unfulfilled desires, back when I used to think these were the ones qui ne valent pas d'être vécus. The latter I saw one day in October, after the leaves had fallen upon the boardwalk sprayed with salt and sand, and the summer had long sung its last chord. I had not realized it was him, then:

The emptiness of the quay along the plage (of the variegated amusement park kind) is hollow, and it is somewhat troubling: the forms and lines of people and their singular movements that occupy the day are gone, and had left us only with the damp movement of the emptiness of their voices. Flyers drifting where they had once been tacked on, and shriveled leaves crackle despite the life, in full color, that they once contained. I am walking alone on the quay, surprised by the rather monotone odor of everything, the graying cold that left no desire for questioning, shrouded in its own sort of sleepless fog. There is one silhouette along the side of the planks close to me, cautiously but confidently moving in preordained rhythm by the planks beneath the curb; he is hunched over in an old shirt and old cap. He doesn't show his face, but he is sweeping the brittle leaves away, into the sewers, into the sinews of his broom. The shuffle of his feet along the sweep echoes that of the leaves, or of the parish in a church, a movement so characteristic of the unthinking stubbornness of old men. He doesn't say much, but it's clear he doesn't want to show his face; he sweeps away slowly, as if his back hurt a bit from old age—he is a diligent sweeper and where he'll sweep they'll disappear forever, to leave those well-traveled streets empty once again, this time not devoid of meaning, but simply forgotten. (What a strange world, For-gotten. Didn't you see my picking at the forget-me-nots when I thought about you? It is a strange word; too long to be forgotten.)

And it had suddenly occurred to me, that I had been there, in that place, once before. That summer I went away, to escape, and perhaps to forget. Except this time it was erasing me, and not I erasing them.

Time the Street Sweeper, where are you now? Unlike what they all wrongly believed. It is not you who heals by picking up the pieces; it is you who sweeps them away. A disappearing act all on its own. Perhaps you are entertaining yourself with them somewhere: little yellow canaries caught by the wires of your leaden cage, your room decadent with little antique souvenirs that once were never yours, and mine barren where I had once stood.

Perhaps all the better to keep it clean.

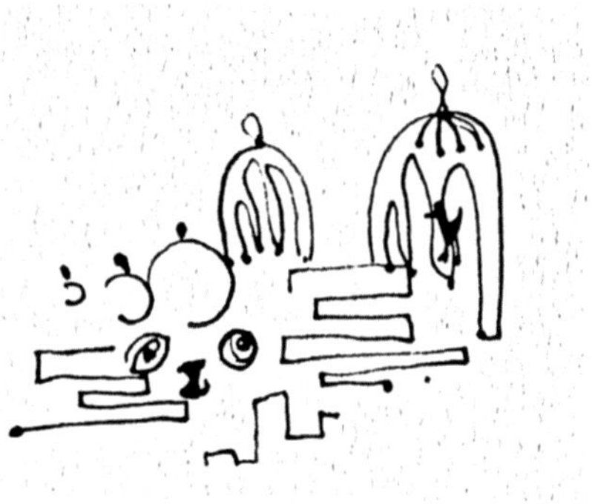

Coda

…and the electric shiver of neon lights,
as I look back to the dry crackle of that summer day, somewhere found and somewhere lost,
in the desert of my consciousness.

Once more, the door opens, closes, as if it knew, soft soundless screen and leaves, that this was not the entr'acte but the conclusion;

Somewhere close the hunter goes, leaves without trees, stars without oceans, wings without feathers, the bow and the spear, in search of something not sunk like Atlantis but ever, ever so rare; it took the form of crystallized thought and the laughter of rain, as the clouds set open the flowers…cut them, bruised them, leaving them susceptible, their skin more tender than they were soft, just like ours the way we gave ourselves open to love…

For isn't that the only way, the sweetest form, loose wandering smells that arise from odorless tears, grows, the fragrance of storms?

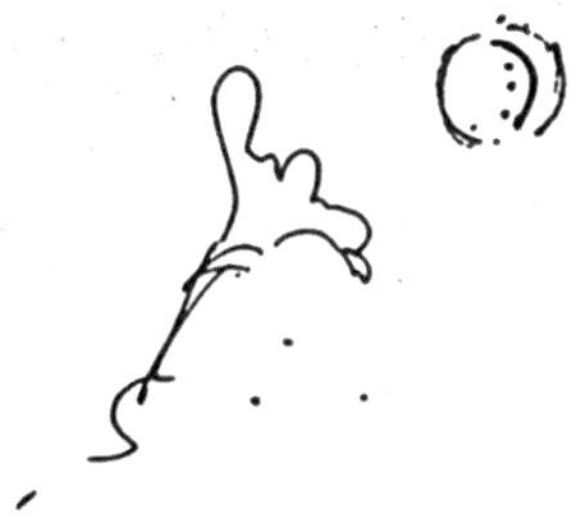

Unity...

For what is form without unity?

Yet perhaps we need to separate things before we can put them back together,
heartstrings, mindcaves,
everything.